*f*P

CINDY IN IRAQ

A CIVILIAN'S YEAR IN THE WAR ZONE

CYNTHIA I. MORGAN

FREE PRESS

NEW YORK LONDON TORONTO SYDNEY

*f*P

FREE PRESS
A Division of Simon & Schuster, Inc.
1230 Avenue of the Americas
New York, NY 10020

FREE PRESS and colophon are
trademarks of Simon & Schuster, Inc.

For information about special discounts for bulk purchases,
please contact Simon & Schuster Special Sales: 1-800-456-6798 or
business@simonandschuster.com

Designed by Davina Mock

Manufactured in the United States of America

1 3 5 7 9 10 8 6 4 2

Library of Congress Cataloging-in-Publication
Data Control Number: 2006040630

ISBN-13: 978-0-7432-8640-4
ISBN-10:   0-7432-8640-5

To my boys, Kenny, Ian, and Steffan—
you are what kept me going when I had lost all hope,
and you are what drives me today to be a better person.
I love ya'll.

CINDY IN IRAQ

PROLOGUE

S O THIS IS WHAT IT'S LIKE TO
be alone.

It was September 20, 2003, and I was sitting in an
airport in Houston, dialing the numbers of friends I'd
known for most of my life. They had seen me struggle,

they had seen me in despair, and now they were talking me through one of the most difficult decisions of my life.

I was going to Iraq. Just a couple of days earlier, in a training camp for new Halliburton employees who were bound for Iraq and Afghanistan, I was given a flak jacket and a helmet and told to get ready to fly. And now I was waiting for that flight, which would take me to Germany, and then to a base in Kuwait. From there, I'd be crossing the border into Iraq and hauling supplies to our troops. I'd be riding in convoys through hostile territory, sleeping behind the wire in our bases and camps throughout the country, and then heading back to Kuwait to do it all over again.

The pay was good—eighty to ninety grand, tax free. Don't think that wasn't an incentive. I had struggled financially all my life. I had been on welfare. I had even given up custody of my three darling boys because I couldn't provide for them. They had been living with their father, my first ex-husband, for years now. Compared to that decision—to give up my kids, my world—going to Iraq was easy.

But I wasn't going to Iraq for the money. I wish it was that simple.

Some of my friends said I should back out now, before I got on that airplane. Some of them didn't say that, but I could tell that's what they were thinking.

How was I going to do this? I was leaving behind the

people I love, going overseas for the first time in my life at age thirty-seven. I'd spent my entire adult life with somebody, be it a friend, a lover, or a husband. I was never truly alone.

But now I was, alone in an airport with strangers who would board the airplane with me. We all were heading for a war zone, to drive trucks in one of the most dangerous places in the world.

While I became friendly with some of my new colleagues, they weren't my old friends, the friends who saw me through three marriages, through the birth of my boys. Maybe I'd get to know these new friends even better once we were in Iraq. Or maybe I'd never see them again, or only in passing. Maybe some of them wouldn't make it back alive. While we were training and waiting in Houston, a Halliburton employee was shot and killed in Iraq. Some of the people I was training with knew him well. In fact, he had recruited them. Several of them went home when they got the news.

It was time to call my boys. Kenneth Wayne was nineteen, Ian Douglas was seventeen, and Steffan Nicholas was fifteen. I had all three of them before I was twenty-three years old. I tried so hard to make a home for them after my husband, Ken, and I split up for good. We lived in Arkansas, and I worked as a waitress, I worked in a chicken processing plant, and when I had to, I went on welfare. I hated that, but I had to do it.

But one terrible day when the boys were six, four, and two, I realized I couldn't do it anymore.

After months of juggling jobs, getting very little sleep, and trying to be the best mom I could be, things seemed to be looking up. It was the beginning of the month, so my food stamps had come in. I went out shopping and bought enough to fill the freezer and the kitchen. We'd have enough to get us through the month.

The next morning, I woke up when I heard some strange noises in the kitchen. The boys were giggling, and I could hear them banging pots and pans. What were they up to?

I got out of bed and went toward all the noise. And there, in the kitchen, were my three beautiful boys, and a month's worth of food scattered all around. "Look, Mommy," Kenny said. "We made you breakfast."

Almost every bit of food in the house was ruined. I had no way to feed them for a month. I had nothing!

The poor kids—they were expecting me to smile and laugh, but I couldn't fake it. I was so furious I had to walk out of the apartment—if I stayed in that kitchen, I was afraid I'd hurt the boys.

I wanted to die, right then and there. I couldn't do this anymore. I was messing up my life, and theirs.

My boys were all I had in the world. They kept me going. They made me smile when smiles were hard to come by. They were my reason for living.

But now I had no way to feed them for a month. It occurred to me that I might be doing them more harm than good by having them live with me. I couldn't take care of myself, never mind my children. So I called my ex-husband, Ken, and asked him to take the boys. I figured my life was ending—my body just hadn't figured it out yet.

Ken agreed, and said he'd have his parents come over to pick them up. My ex in-laws arrived soon afterward, and they packed the boys and their bags into their van. It was horrible—the worst day of my life. Kenny, who was six, realized what was happening and he started screaming when he got into the van. It ripped out my heart. It took all my strength and determination not to run after them, gather them up in my arms, and tell them that we'd never be apart.

But I couldn't do it.

I had decided the boys would be better off with their father, who lived in Helena, Arkansas. I get teary-eyed even now, fifteen years later, when I think about that day.

I can still hear Kenny screaming as he left. My former in-laws took them away in their van, and my heart broke.

I called them from the airport, and I asked them one last time if they were okay with my going to Iraq. My friends couldn't talk me out of it, but my boys could have. But they all said they supported my decision, and that they loved me. I'm not sure how long I cried after I hung up, but it was a good long while. What if I didn't make it home? How would they handle that?

I had to put that possibility out of my mind. I would be coming back. I had to come back.

Then it was time to make one last call: to my third ex-husband, Bill. Nine months earlier, Bill had tried to kill me in a motel room in Ogden, Utah. He put his hands around my throat and tried to choke me. Somehow I got free and called the cops, and Bill was put briefly in jail. And, damn it, I still loved him.

We were both truck drivers, and our marriage had been filled with all kinds of conflict. But I believed he loved me. I tried to leave him, but I couldn't—until now.

I dialed his number, and he picked up. He did his best to tell me I shouldn't go. He wanted to know if I really had to go halfway around the world—to a war—to get away from him. As much as I wanted to tell him the truth, I lied. I told him I wasn't trying to get away from him.

I knew he'd never get over the guilt if I got killed and

he thought it was because I was trying to get away from him. I knew that somehow, he still loved me, just like I loved him.

Just like when we were married, I wound up trying to support him. Here I was going to a place where I might get shot, where I could die, and I ended up being supportive of Bill, instead of the other way around.

But I knew I had to go. I had to get him out of my system. If I didn't, I would die—maybe not physically, but spiritually, and I don't know which would be worse.

I said good-bye, and I hung up the phone. It was time to board the plane. Next stop: Germany, followed by Kuwait City.

As my plane approached the Middle East, the pilot got on the public address system and told us which country we were flying over. That's when all of this became real to me—I had really left Arkansas, I had really left my kids and my friends and Bill and my life as I knew it. I was about to enter another country, another culture. I was nervous and excited at the same time.

The plane made an arc over the Persian Gulf. I could

see the twinkling of colorful lights in the distance. It was an unexpected sight, like seeing flowers in a desert.

What in all hell was I doing here?

If there's a war on, you can be pretty certain that somebody in my family is in the middle of it. My great-grandfather on my mother's side fought in World War I. His daughter, my maternal grandmother, served in the Women's Air Corps as a flight instructor during World War II. Her brothers—my great-uncles—fought in Korea, and his grandson, my mother's brother, fought in Vietnam. My brother joined the Navy in 1987, which actually gave my mother a sense of relief. She figured he was safe because he was on a submarine. You can't get a sub to Iraq, she said. But her relief turned to dread when my oldest son joined the Army not long after 9/11.

And then, in August of 2003, I told her that I was on my way to war, too. I signed up with a subsidiary of Halliburton—Kellogg, Brown and Root, or KBR. I wasn't necessarily following in the tradition of other family members, in the sense that I wasn't joining the military. But I was going to a war all the same, and I would be part of the largest deployment of civilian contractors in any war, anywhere.

Yes, I would be well paid for the work, and if I could do it for a few years, I'd be financially secure for the first time in my life. I'd be able to buy my own truck, instead of constantly leasing one.

I wanted to serve my country, too. I told my family that I was going to Iraq so I could help the troops, just like somebody else might help my son if he found himself in Iraq as well.

Ultimately, though, I just had to get away. From Bill. From my old life. I knew that once I set foot in the Middle East, I would never be the same person again. And that was exactly what I wanted.

ONE

WE CALLED OUR APARTMENT complex in Kuwait the "twin towers." They weren't nearly as tall as the Twin Towers were—these were just nineteen stories high—but just saying the words reminded us of why we were there. Terrorists took down the Twin Towers in New York, and we were in the twin towers in Kuwait, helping our troops take down the terrorists.

The apartments in the towers had two regular bedrooms, a master bedroom, and a maid's quarters. I managed to get the maid's quarters, so I had nobody else in my room and I had my own shower. Other contractors doubled up in the regular bedrooms. It was a little cramped, although nobody seemed to mind. We were too focused on the mission, and besides, whatever the conditions were in Kuwait, we had it better than the troops did.

The first few days in Kuwait were weird. Although I was now thousands of miles away from my family and friends, it wasn't like I was out of touch. I strolled over to an Internet café near the towers, paid twenty dollars for ten hours of Internet access, and sent emails and instant messages to the folks back home. I had a digital camera with me, so I was able to email pictures of the spectacular sunsets and sunrises over the Persian Gulf. Back when my uncle was in Vietnam and my great-uncles were in Korea, they'd have to wait weeks for a letter from home. Now, although I wasn't yet in a combat zone, I was just an Internet connection away from my friends and family.

Just in case I forgot where I was, though, there was plenty to remind me that I was in a dangerous place, doing dangerous work. As I got to know some other drivers, I heard talk that the trucks we'd be driving might have to be outfitted with armor. In fact, I heard that as an experiment, KBR put armor on a truck and shot it up to see whether it worked. I sure hoped it did, although our biggest concern was not bullets but rocks. We heard that some of the locals in Iraq were in the habit of throwing big rocks and bricks at our trucks.

That was just the first hint of what we might face. During our briefings, we were told that Iraqi children might lie down in front of our trucks to slow down the convoys or prevent us from moving forward, but under no circumstances should we stop—we should put our trucks in the lowest gear and keep moving, slowly. The kids, we were told, would get out of the way when they realized we weren't going to stop. I couldn't imagine being in that position: playing chicken with a bunch of kids. I didn't know what I'd do if it came to that.

I was running on adrenaline when I first got to Kuwait, but pretty soon I realized that something was wrong. It was hot—well over a hundred degrees—and I kept drinking water, but it went right through me. I wasn't sweating like I should. One of the company's safety officers told me I looked tired.

After three or four days, I came down with what everybody called Kuwaiti crud. My sinuses were killing me and I was coughing my head off. I had gotten my anthrax and smallpox shots the day before, and whether or not the two were related, I didn't know. All I knew was that I felt awful. I struggled through some more training sessions and a defensive driving class. More than anything else, I just wanted to get to work. I was tired of sitting around. I wanted to be on the road.

I had started driving not long after the boys went to live with their father. I rode for three months with a driver friend, just to clear my head. When the trip was over, I decided this was something I could do, and something I'd like. My friend had warned me that trucking was a living, but it wasn't a life. Of course, if he didn't think I should get behind the wheel, that was the wrong argument to make. I was tired of the life I was leading anyway.

I asked another friend who drove to teach me everything he knew. He did, and during one ride, as we drove near Texarkana, he pulled out the throttle—sort of a truck driver's way of kicking in cruise control—and told me to get behind the wheel. I freaked, but I did it. And while I was driving toward Dallas, my friend didn't sit in the cab with me—he went to the bunk and fell asleep. That's how much confidence he had in me. That confidence gave me some confidence of my own.

I went to driving school, where I was one of only three women. After finishing the ten-week course in the summer of 1991, I applied for a job in a Georgia-based outfit. I dropped off my application on a hot August day. One of the dispatchers asked me if I could take a road test right away. "Of course," I said, without thinking. The dispatcher asked a couple of the guys if one of them would get in the truck with me for the test. Two of them refused, but one of them said that if I could get his truck out of the yard safely, he'd supervise my road test. I was nervous, and during the walk to his truck, the driver said that I didn't look like a female truck driver.

I snapped back: "Well, this is what a female truck driver looks like, because that's what I am." He smiled and said we'd get along fine.

I got the job, but it wasn't always easy. Being a woman, I knew I had to be ten times as good as the guys, and that I'd have to fight for anything I wanted. I had to fight to get long hauls, because some of the men figured that boring short hauls were women's work. But the fight was worth it, because I succeeded. I was a damn good truck driver, and I loved it.

My family didn't understand. First, I sent the boys to live with Ken. They didn't understand that. And when I started driving, they thought I was giving up on the boys completely. But it was just the opposite: I hoped that with a job that paid decent money, I'd be able to bring the boys back. That was my goal. But it didn't happen, and that is my biggest regret. Although I saw them whenever a haul brought me near Ken's house near Memphis (sometimes, I picked them up from school in my truck), they never returned to live with me.

After meeting with my supervisor in Kuwait, I asked to drive a refrigerated truck, known in the trade as a "reefer." I had driven reefers in the States for a while. Refrigerated trucks, as you would expect, haul ice and perishable products, like meat and vegetables. It turned out that there was a shortage of reefer drivers, so I figured volunteering to drive one was my best chance to get on the road quickly.

As for the trucks themselves, they were awful. Most of them were European-made, with little differences that required big adjustments—like convex mirrors instead of flat mirrors, which threw off our depth perception when backing up. Mechanically, they were just plain junk. We weren't assigned trucks. We grabbed what was available, and I learned pretty quickly that if I found a truck with halfway decent brakes and a little air-conditioning, I should grab it, because that was about the best I could do. Eventually we got better trucks, just in time to start getting shot at.

While we awaited our first mission, we were on lockdown in the towers, which meant that we couldn't go into Kuwait City on our down time. But if we were assigned a local mission, like loading ice, we got a chance to see a little local color. We all loved being asked to go to the icehouse, because it was right beside a fish market and the Shark Mall.

Finally, on September 28, 2003, I got word that I'd be part of a convoy leaving for Iraq the following morning.

I had to get up at four o'clock in the morning to catch a shuttle bus from the twin towers to our staging area. The shuttle bus never appeared. I was stuck at the towers while my first convoy was waiting for me. I called my foreman, a British guy named Andy, and he seemed to understand, but once I finally showed up, Andy hammered me. This was my first fucking mission, and I was fucking late, and did I understand how fucking important it was to be on time. I figured I was done for, but one of the other guys took me aside and told me he could tell Andy liked me. If he didn't, he would have sent me back to the towers and found another driver to replace me. Instead, he just chewed me out and then we got on with business. Andy was one of the few foremen I met who really seemed to care about his drivers and what they needed. Of course, I didn't find that out until I worked for him for a while.

We pulled out at 9:50 A.M. We had thirteen trucks in

the convoy—three of us were employees of KBR, and we were hauling ice. None of us had driven in Iraq before. Nine other drivers were what we called TCNs—third-country nationals—who were working for other contractors. They were hauling food. Rounding out the convoy was the convoy commander, a guy I'll call Jack, who didn't haul a trailer. In the trucking business, that's known as "running bobtail." The CC's job was to make sure we stayed together and stayed in line. I was third in line, and Jack put himself behind me; when we approached checkpoints, he would pull out and get in front of the convoy.

The Iraqi border was about a two-hour ride from our staging area. Our eventual destination was Camp Sycamore, which was near Tikrit, Saddam's home town and the center of his power base. The ride would take a couple of days.

We crossed the border into Iraq at 12:55 P.M. As I feared, there were children everywhere along the roadside, but none of them got in front of the trucks. I was relieved—I really didn't know what I'd do if they had decided to lie down in front of me. These kids just wanted some food, or shoes—anything we could give them. It was heartbreaking to see these young kids in bare feet, walking across hot sand. How could Saddam have allowed his people to live like this?

For all my anxiety, the first part of our ride was uneventful, except for the sand. There was no escaping it, and there was nothing else. Imagine driving in the deserts of the American Southwest. Now, take away the hills, the occasional town, the other cars on the highway, add a little sand, and you have an idea of what this ride was like. You feel as though you've reached the end of the earth. We pulled into a camp called Cedar 2, which was nicknamed, with good reason, the Dust Bowl. It was in the middle of the desert, about two and a half hours north of the Kuwaiti border. Even though the ancient city of Ur was nearby, as was the Tallil air base, you got a tremendous feeling of isolation there. At the time, Cedar was a major Army camp, although it later became a center for KBR contractors. Because of its strategic location between the border and Baghdad, it was a major fueling point for convoys and a safe haven at night.

After we pulled in, I wanted a shower. But getting one wasn't that simple in a war zone. The camp had community showers—and I had missed the time set aside for women to use them. But the camp manager took pity on me and told Jack to clear out the shower area and stand guard by the door while I took a shower. That was cool. The manager even had somebody drive me back to my truck after my shower, so I wouldn't get all dusty again.

Here, in this isolated post in an isolated desert, wouldn't you know it—I ran into a friend from home, a guy named Keith who was in the National Guard. It was

Keith who had told me about job openings at Halliburton months earlier, when I was looking to get away from Bill and my old life. If he hadn't told me, I don't know what I would have done.

Keith actually spotted me before I saw him. I was on my way to breakfast when I heard a familiar voice. Keith was doubly surprised to see me. First of all, you don't expect to run into friends in the middle of the Iraqi desert. Plus, nobody ever told him that I decided to take a job in Iraq. We had a great chat, and he warned me to be careful. "I want to see that cute butt of yours all in one piece," he said.

The following morning we pushed out before six o'clock. I drove at the head of the convoy, which I liked because I could actually see something other than the back of a truck. What I saw from the front was similar to what I had seen the day before—kids, some of them as young as four or five, begging for food, for clothes, for anything. Some of them were holding empty packages that had contained ready-made meals—called MREs (Meals Ready to Eat) in military lingo—which our troops had. They were begging for more. We stopped at one point, and I took pictures of two boys and gave them a bottle of water from my truck. As much as I wanted to stop and talk to them, we had been told that we should never get out of our trucks.

I was in tears when we started moving again. No matter what people were saying at home, the sight of those kids convinced me that we did the right thing by coming over here. Saddam lived in a palace with gold shitters, while the children of his country starved. I wished the people back home could see what I was seeing.

We stopped again for the night at a refueling point in Scania, about an hour and a half south of Baghdad. The camp was very basic. No showers—the troops took what they called bottle showers. They'd find a private spot somewhere in camp and douse themselves with bottled water. They lived in tents and ate MREs. I was happy that we didn't spend much time there.

The following morning we loaded up and set out for our final destination on this trip, Camp Sycamore, via Baghdad. I found myself looking at the endless blue horizon in front of me. There wasn't a cloud in the sky. In fact, it had been a while since I had seen a cloud. It's funny, I never thought I'd miss something so ordinary as the clouds.

Our drive through Baghdad was not nearly as pleasant as a clear blue sky. This was my first trip to the city. It stank. Literally. It was filthy, with garbage piled up in the middle of streets. Parts of it admittedly were beautiful, especially the mosques. But most of the buildings were run-down, and I got the feeling that this had nothing to do with the war. The city had suffered just like the Iraqi people had suffered during Saddam's regime. The streets were full of contradictions. I saw carts being pulled by donkeys and horses, and then I'd see a Mercedes-Benz squeezing through a narrow lane. Parts of the city were old and decrepit; parts were new and modern.

Camp Sycamore, like the camp at Scania, was pretty rough. I was hot and dusty again, and I wanted a shower. They had one, if you could call it that, near the area where trucks unloaded and loaded their stuff. The stall was a bunch of boards nailed together to make a box, with no roof. A water bag hung from a board on top of the stall.

Since the stall had no roof, I wasn't about to take a shower while it was daylight. I didn't want anybody peeking in. Some of the guys suggested that I wait until it was dark. That sounded like a good idea, but what they didn't tell me was that the water in the water bag wasn't heated, except by the sun. I should have been a little suspicious when some of the guys decided to join Jack in standing guard by the stall while I showered. Sure enough, I dumped the water on me and let out a scream. The water was freezing! I heard Jack and the other guys laughing their tails off. It does seem funny now, but it wasn't at the time. I swore I wouldn't fall for something like that again.

We had some beer, and then Jack walked me to my truck, where I'd be sleeping. He asked me for a kiss. I saw this one coming a mile away. "Aren't you married?" I asked.

"Yes and no," he said. Yes and no—what was that

supposed to mean? I gave him a hug instead. I didn't leave home to go through all that crap again.

As blue as the sky was a few hours earlier, it was pitch-black now, except for the stars. I'd never seen so many. After Jack left, I stood outside the truck and just watched the sky. It was eleven at night in Iraq, so it was about three o'clock in the afternoon back home in Arkansas. They say it's a small world, but on a night like this one, the world felt huge, and home seemed a million miles away.

Just before Jack left, I told him that I didn't expect to be the same person in a year, when my contract expired. "You've already changed, just by deciding to come here," he said. "Even if you went home tomorrow, after only one convoy, you'd be a different person."

I believed him.

Damn, I missed my boys.

After unloading our stuff at Sycamore, we joined up with an Army tanker convoy headed for Camp Anaconda, about an hour north of Baghdad, on October 2. The bosses at KBR didn't like us to run with military convoys, because they were coming under attack more often than civilian convoys. And running with not just a military convoy, but with military tanker trucks carrying fuel—well, that only increased the chances of something going wrong. But we were anxious to get to Anaconda, so we pushed the rules a little bit.

Anaconda was a huge camp, a far cry from the outposts we had seen. It had been one of Saddam's bases, and our troops took it over after the old regime fell. We got there just before noon, had real showers, met some of the guys who had flown over from the States with me.

Jack and I wound up dancing at the MWR (Morale, Welfare, and Recreation) together that night. It was just Jack and me—and a bunch of young soldiers. It was really great to watch these young kids, some of them Kenny's age, having a good time. By day, they carried M-16s and were in harm's way. But at night they had a chance to relax and have a little fun.

Most people back home don't think much about what soldiers do when they're not on patrol or fighting the enemy. I certainly never gave it a thought. That night in Anaconda, I saw a hidden side of war—I saw our troops enjoying themselves, relaxing, having fun. It changed the way I saw the life of a soldier, and knowing that my son Kenny had just finished boot camp, I took some comfort in seeing these brave men and women having a few moments of fun and companionship.

Jack wasn't much of a dancer, but we had fun, too. Afterward, we went outside with some of the other contractors to watch a lightning show in the Iraqi sky. It was awesome, and then, as an added attraction, some mortars started falling nearby. I wanted to stay and watch, but a camp guard approached and said we had to go to the bunker.

"Do we have to?" I asked. I really didn't want to leave.

"Ma'am," he said—the soldiers were so polite—"I just have to ask you to go to a bunker."

"Okay," I said. I got up and sat down again. Jack and the other guys thought that was funny, so they stayed with me. I wasn't going to miss this for the world, and besides, I didn't think we were in any real danger. So I stayed and watched, and I even dug out some shrapnel that was embedded in a building nearby to keep as a souvenir.

Throughout my first few weeks in Iraq, I was in constant touch with everybody back home. With a laptop and a digital camera, I not only could send and receive emails, but I could also send pictures home. I set up a website, which my sister Mary managed. She posted pictures of me, along with my emails home. Pretty soon I was hearing from people all over the States.

We left Anaconda for Cedar 2 on October 5, traveling the same road we had been on before, code-named MSR Tampa. As usual, we drove at about sixty miles an hour, which, considering the conditions and the dangers, was pretty damn slow. We would have been driving a lot faster back home, I can tell you. But we weren't supposed to drive faster than 100 kilometers an hour, which is a little more than sixty miles an hour.

It was a pretty uneventful trip, until we reached a town just to the north of Cedar 2. The drivers call the place "Rockville," and I quickly found out why. As I approached a burned-out flatbed along the roadside—a reminder of just how dangerous this job could be—a huge rock came out of nowhere and hit my windshield. It left a huge indentation on the passenger's side. Then three more rocks hit the truck. I never saw who threw them.

As we were pulling into Cedar 2, Jack contacted me via CB radio. He had gotten a message, asking me to contact a supervisor at headquarters. I had a terrible feeling about this. I called the supervisor from a satellite phone in camp and was told that I was to be on the first convoy headed south the following morning. Something was up—I knew it. I asked the supervisor if this had anything to do with my grandfather, Papaw. He didn't say anything, and I kept pushing him until he finally told me: Papaw had died.

I had no intention of going home. The supervisor seemed shocked. That's why they put me on that convoy going south. They figured I'd want to get back to Kuwait City and go home. I explained that I had had a long talk with my grandparents before I left, and Papaw told me if anything happened to him while I was away, I should stay put and help the troops. I had every intention of living up to his wishes.

Papaw had been my rock for so many years, and right before I left for Iraq, my mother took me aside and said: "You know, you're the apple of Papaw's eye." That meant so much to me. He was proud of me for going to Iraq— he and Mamaw seemed to understand more than anybody else why I was doing this, and why it was important not just to me, but for our troops and for our country. And yet, by being in Iraq, I was thousands of miles away when Papaw died. Although I knew what Papaw wanted, I felt helpless. There was a part of me that wanted to go home, so I could be there for Mamaw.

As upset as I was, I had to take care of business. My foreman had some questions for me about getting rocked. He figured I might be too scared to drive for a while, but if I seemed upset, it was because of the news about Papaw. I told the foreman I was fine and that I was ready to get on the road again. He told me I was a tough woman, because some drivers went home after getting rocked. I couldn't believe that—how could a few rocks send you home?

The following morning I was part of a convoy headed from Cedar 2 to Baghdad International Airport, known as BIAP. I didn't drive—Jack, my friend and the convoy commander, decided that I was too upset to be at the wheel, so I rode with another driver.

On our way to BIAP, we pulled into Camp Scania to refuel. Because the camp was rudimentary and small, as we lined up to leave the base, we were staged on the road outside the camp perimeter. In some places, this would be an invitation to attack, but conditions were relatively safe near Scania.

Our convoys did attract the attention of some of the local Iraqi children, who crowded around us, trying to sell stuff or talk us into giving them something—food, clothes, anything. I noticed that most of the children were barefoot. The soles of their feet looked like leather from walking on hot sand and asphalt. In the States, if a child's feet looked like that, a parent would go to jail for child abuse. But for these kids, it was normal. They were poor, and their clothes were dirty and worn-out.

One little boy named Adgnon stole my heart. He was nine years old, spunky, and lovable. He and his brother,

Ida, must have been luckier than the rest: Their hair was clean. Most of the other boys looked like they hadn't had a bath in a long time. Somebody clearly was trying to do his or her best for these two boys.

Adgnon reminded me of my youngest, Steffan. When he thought the other kids were giving me a hard time, trying to sell me something, he let them have it—he had a pretty foul mouth, but it was funny. He didn't speak much English and could understand even less, but I communicated with him through his brother or with one of the other boys. Or we just used sign language.

I gave Adgnon my Peterbilt cap and a wink. He asked me what that meant. "It means I like you," I said. His friends got such a kick out of that! They were whooping and teasing him. Another one of the boys took Jack aside and wanted to know if he could buy me. He offered a hundred dollars "for the missus." That really tickled me. I took some pictures before we set out for the BIAP, and as we drove off, the kids were blowing kisses at us. I hoped I would see Adgnon again on the road.

We arrived at the BIAP staging area at about two o'clock that afternoon. My family back home were gathering to say good-bye to Papaw, and I wasn't there to mourn with them. I was so distracted that I sort of stumbled out of the truck. As I regained my footing, I looked down and saw a rock shaped like a heart. It was a gift from Papaw, a sign of his love for me and mine for him.

Suddenly I felt at peace. I no longer felt guilty about missing the funeral, because I had a piece of Papaw's love with me.

In early October, I was part of a twenty-five-truck convoy assigned to haul food, produce, milk, and ice from Kuwait City to the airport near Baghdad. It was an important mission—until now, we had been hauling only ice, but now we were going to try to haul food and other perishable goods. There was also a sense that this mission could be dangerous—hauling food made us a more valuable target for terrorists, and we were traveling the hazardous road to BIAP and the military camps nearby. Joining us for the ride were some military police and a truck armed with a .50-caliber machine gun.

I loved going to BIAP, because it was a lot more than just an airport. It was almost a self-contained city. The Air Force had a camp there, and the Army had several. With all of these troops and contractors together, the BIAP was a happening place. Soldiers and contractors mingled freely, without brass and bosses looking over our shoulders. We'd get together for cookouts. We'd make a fire out of some of the discarded pallets and throw a metal door over the blaze. Then we'd pile chicken, steaks, and pork chops on the door. That was the only way we could cook so much meat—talk about necessity being the mother of invention! Yes—we cooked the meat on a metal door.

It wouldn't be a cookout without stories, and I heard dozens from other contractors who had seen it all and then some. Alcohol helped the storytelling process. Drinking was against company policy, but of course we drank—we were in a war in the middle of the desert. Red Bull and vodka was a big favorite.

Sometimes soldiers joined us, and we always shared our food and company with the men and women who were bearing the brunt of this war.

On this particular trip, we didn't get off to a very promising start. A truck broke down before we even got out of Kuwait City, and Jack had to stay with the stranded driver. He assigned me the job of leading the rest of the convoy to Camp Navistar, on the border between Kuwait and Iraq. All convoys passed through Navistar. Since I had made the trip several times before, I knew the way, but having responsibility for so many people was a big deal, and even in Kuwait, you never knew what or who might be on the roadside waiting for you.

I don't know how many women were leading convoys on a regular basis, but it certainly was unusual. I wasn't an official convoy commander, or even an assistant, so I felt even more pressure. We weren't on the road very long when another truck broke down. One of the other drivers had my cell phone number and called me to let me know what had happened. The cell phones came in handy—we weren't allowed to use CB radios because they cluttered the airwaves. Each convoy commander and the driver at the back of each convoy carried handheld radios, which we tried to use sparingly because the batteries didn't last very long.

I called Jack on his cell, and he told us to go ahead without the driver, because he was on his way. I was relieved to get to Navistar without any further incidents, and even more relieved when Jack showed up. I know the other drivers wanted their CC in charge. It wasn't so much that I was a woman, they just wanted somebody who knew the ropes, because an inexperienced CC could get you in trouble, and a good CC could get you out of trouble.

On another leg of the trip, we had more mechanical problems when a truck lost its transmission. We all pulled over to the side of the road. Out of nowhere, that .50-caliber machine gun went off and ripped open a huge hole in one of our trailers. It was an accident, and the driver wasn't hurt, but for a few minutes people were pretty scared. The damaged trailer had to be examined to find an exit wound. Well, there was none, which means the bullets never made it past the ice inside the trailer. Somebody's Coke was going to be served with a little extra ingredient!

As we approached Baghdad, we were brought to a halt when an Army patrol ahead of us spotted a makeshift roadside bomb—known in the trade as an "improvised explosive device" or IED—ahead of us. IEDs were becoming a real hazard to the troops and to contractors like us. We waited more than two hours in the middle of a road outside Baghdad, which wasn't the safest place to be, until the troops set off the bomb out of harm's way. I saw dust flying in the distance.

After a two-day trip, we finally made it to the airport on October 14. Along the way, we stopped to refuel at Camp Scania, and as we staged outside the camp, I saw my little boyfriend, Adgnon, on the roadside, along with his brother, Ida, who was wearing the Peterbilt cap I gave him. Adgnon was wearing a ring, and he took it off with some effort, reached up into my truck, and gave it to me as a gift. Ida asked me if I could get Adgnon some shoes. When some older boys came along, Adgnon acted like he was my protector—he made sure none of the boys came close to my truck, just in case they were up to no good.

I didn't know what to say when Ida asked me if I could take Adgnon to America. I only wished that I could show him what life was like outside of Iraq. Some MPs came by and started shooing away the boys. I tried to get them to leave Adgnon alone, but they had their job to do. As we started rolling, Adgnon ran along a dirt road on our right, scrambled up a pile of dirt, and blew me a kiss. Watching him run down that road after us broke my heart. I don't pray very much, but that day I prayed for Adgnon.

After we got to the airport, I went shopping for Adgnon. I bought him a pair of shoes, along with some socks. I bought his brother a few shirts. On our way back south, when we staged outside Scania after refueling, I looked for the two of them amid the crowd of boys along the roadside. Since my last visit, the military had strung barbed wire along the road where we staged, so even if I found the boys, it was going to be hard to give them their presents.

I asked the other boys if they knew where Adgnon was. Some of them spoke English, or enough to get by. One of them said Adgnon was sick. Another said he thought Adgnon was at home. I asked if somebody would go and find him. Adgnon showed up a few minutes later with a big smile on his face.

I wanted to hug him but I couldn't. The concertina wire kept us apart. My shirt got hung up on the barbs as I passed a bag filled with shoes, shirts, and other things through the wire. Adgnon didn't even look at what was inside the bag. He looked at me, and his eyes said it all. He had tears in his eyes. He reached forward like he wanted to hug me, but the damned wire was between us. Then he turned away and left, probably because he didn't want his friends to see him crying.

I did get a chance to ask him what happened to the Peterbilt cap. He said an American soldier had taken it away from them—the two brothers shared the hat, and everything else, it seemed. I couldn't believe it. We were trying to show the Iraqis that we came to liberate them, that we were on their side, and somebody goes and takes a cap from a kid? I swore I'd better not find some soldier wearing that cap.

On October 23, a day after Jack left for R&R in the States, the Army woke us up at five o'clock in the morning. We were in Camp Cedar for the night, after pulling in from Kuwait. It was extremely unusual for the Army to wake us up, which was a sign that something was up. We had to run a small convoy from Cedar to Camp Dogwood, which was a pretty dangerous place. It was a short trip, but nobody was taking any chances. The CC for the trip assigned a shooter—a soldier with a weapon—to ride shotgun with me. I knew why the CC put a shooter with me: He felt he had to "protect" me because I was a woman. I hated that attitude, and I argued with the CC, but there was no changing his mind.

Still, this trip was a victory for me because I was going to ride drag. That meant I would be the last vehicle in the convoy and would be responsible for recovering any trailers that broke down (I would be running bobtail, meaning without a trailer of my own). If we hit an ambush, my job would be to rescue any driver who got hit and couldn't keep driving. That was a very serious responsibility, but it was one I was ready for. As far as I knew, no other woman had run drag before. To his credit, Jack had made this happen. Knowing how much I wanted the assignment, he made sure that I was slotted to run drag on this mission. There was nothing the CC could do about that.

It was ironic, too, that the shooter who rode with me also was a woman. She was married to another soldier who was based in Baghdad, and she told me she had just gotten a chance to see him to celebrate her birthday, which was today. I imagined it was hard for both of them.

She told me that the Army had found three IEDs along the road earlier that morning, which may have been why she was there in the truck with me. But the trip passed without incident. I had a chance to enjoy a rare sight in Iraq—an island of green grass amid the unending sea of brown sand. The area was rumored to be near the Garden of Eden.

Once we got into camp, we found out that the brass had nowhere to put the ice we brought, and had no need for the food we had. In fact, they had two trailers' worth of rotting produce. Two of their refrigerated trailers weren't working, a third barely worked, and one was fine. This was infuriating. We had come all the way to this camp with ice, and there was no place to put it? Ridiculous. I came up with an idea: Dump the rotten produce and burn it, and then put our two trailers of ice into their one working refrigeration unit.

The CC shrugged his shoulders. If it had been up to him, he'd have turned around with the ice and left. That would have been just plain stupid—the camp had been without ice for four days. Even though it wasn't my job, I was determined to get that ice off the trucks. I asked around for help, and one of the drivers said he didn't come to Iraq to unload produce. So I and another woman, a Jamaican-born soldier, got to work. We got some help dumping one load of produce, but we were on our own for the second. Finally we got some real help unloading the ice into the good reefer. It was hard work, and I was exhausted when it was done, but I felt good knowing we did what we had to do for the sake of our troops.

Later that night, after I took a shower and went to the PX, the camp went into blackout. That was standard procedure so we wouldn't be an easy target in the dark of night. I was with a friend, and we were pretty far from the area where we were being staged—Camp Dogwood was huge. We had to get back to the staging area, so I jumped into my truck and drove across part of the camp with nothing but my clearance lights on. My friends thought I was nuts, but I loved it. It was sort of like being a kid, doing something on the edge that you know is dangerous, but damn, what a rush!

It felt good to feel good. For a change. It felt like I really was becoming that person I was looking for when I left Houston.

TWO

WHAT WAS I DOING HERE?

That was the first question I asked myself when I got to the Middle East. What was I doing here? Months later, I was troubled by another question, which I was starting to hear over and over: What are *we* doing here? I heard it from the Jamaican woman who helped me unload the trailers at Dogwood. I heard it from other civilians. And I knew people were asking the same question at home. *What were we doing here?*

In late October 2003, I met a thirty-seven-year-old sergeant from Texas. Let's call him Jay. He was on the brink of his third divorce—all three of his wives had left him while he was deployed overseas. Men and women in the military sacrifice a lot—sometimes they make the ultimate sacrifice—for our freedom. But you don't hear much about the price they often pay in terms of ruined marriages and home lives. Jay has sacrificed a great deal to serve his country.

I met Jay in Dogwood. Jay was a civil affairs guy, which meant he'd go out into the towns and villages of Iraq to help build schools—and trust. He had returned recently from building a school in a village somewhere in Iraq. He and his buddies were able to stick around long enough to see the school opened. One of the first things the troops are taught, he said, is that Iraqi women were not to be touched, ever. No innocent hugs—no contact whatsoever.

When Jay and his unit showed up for the school's opening, they were mobbed by the kids. It was great, but Jay said he wasn't necessarily surprised. Kids are kids the world over. They want to learn, and they appreciate people who are willing to help them. The kids just wanted to say thanks to Jay and his guys not only because of the work they did but also because they took time out to talk to the kids and become friendly with them.

The shocking part of the ceremony was the reaction of the school's women teachers. They rushed up to the troops and hugged them! Jay said the troops didn't know what to do. They had been told there was to be no physical contact between male troops and female civilians, but what could they do now with these teachers initiating the contact? Jay said some of the guys were afraid they'd get arrested if they returned the hugs, but the teachers wouldn't let go until they got a hug. It sounded a little awkward, but pretty nice, too.

"We've lost a lot of good men and women in all of this," Jay said, "but the Iraqis lost even more before we even got here. So now we're trying to give back something, something they should have had all along."

Jay said he didn't necessarily feel that way when he first got to Iraq. He didn't have a whole lot of sympathy for the people he saw every day, in part because suicide bombers were mixed in with the general population. You never knew if that Iraqi civilian along the road was just a poor victim of Saddam's reign or a terrorist ready to blow himself up along with as many troops and civilians as possible.

But then one day Jay was working a checkpoint, stopping cars and asking for identification—routine stuff. He noticed a guy in a car waiting on line. The guy looked like he was crying, and he seemed to be reaching for something on the seat next to him.

Of course, Jay immediately suspected that the guy was a suicide bomber who was just realizing what he had gotten himself into. Who wouldn't cry if he was about to blow himself up, and for what?

Jay and the other troops leaped into action. They surrounded the car and ordered the driver to get out with his hands on his head. He did. You can imagine the tension. For all Jay knew, there was a bomb in the car and it was about to go off. The troops saw a box on the passenger's seat. The driver took it out—it was empty, except for a picture of a handsome young man. The driver cried even more now, and kept looking at Jay and saying something in Arabic.

The troops called for an interpreter. When he arrived, the driver explained that the picture in the box was of his son. He had been killed by Saddam's soldiers three weeks before the invasion because he wouldn't join the army. Then he held up the picture. The young man looked just like Jay, only with slightly darker skin. The driver said that when he saw Jay, he burst into tears because of the resemblance to his son. Jay told me that from then on, he had a good deal more compassion for the Iraqi people and all that they've been through. "I started seeing them as people, and not as the enemy," he said.

That attitude changed the way he saw even some Iraqi soldiers. True, some of them were fanatics who were ready to die and kill for Saddam. But some had been forced into service at the point of a gun. After the checkpoint incident, Jay was out on patrol when some Iraqi soldiers approached the column and surrendered. The U.S. troops took away their weapons and let them go home. Their fight was over.

I wished Jay could tell his story to every American who asks: Why are we in Iraq? They needed to know that our troops are doing everything they can to give the Iraqi people a chance at a better life. What was going on in Iraq wasn't just about bombs and gunfire and death. It was about people from two very different countries and cultures coming together to make something good out of something deplorable.

Right around the same time as my talk with Jay, I saw my friend Adgnon along the roadside again. As usual, he was with some of his friends, and like last time, we were separated by that concertina wire strung up along the roads to protect our vehicles.

Adgnon told me through one of the other boys that his father was shot by Saddam's orders because he would not join the Iraqi military. Then he and his brother, Ida, asked me again to take him to America. God, I would have loved to say yes, but I couldn't. We talked for a while, but then it was time to go. He and his friends shook my hand through the concertina wire. I left wishing, hoping, that I could do something to help Adgnon, and all the kids like Adgnon in Iraq.

I wasn't the only woman truck driver in Iraq. Far from it. But still, women truck drivers weren't exactly commonplace. Some of the males didn't know what to make of us, of me. And nothing bothers me more than a male who treats me differently just because I'm a woman.

We caught a convoy in late October running from Dogwood to BIAP. We had military vehicles along with us, but they were all deployed in front of the column. I was supposed to be last in line, running bobtail, just me in the cab.

Our convoy commander for this run, a guy named Ron, told me he preferred to have the military vehicles stacked up in front of the column, as opposed to being interspersed throughout the convoy. Ron, truth be told, was one of the worst CCs I ever ran with. He didn't seem to care about taking the time to set up a proper convoy. He just tacked us on to the end of a military convoy, almost like we were an afterthought.

He certainly didn't think much of the idea of having me at the end of the convoy, and I knew exactly why: Ron didn't think I could handle riding back there with no protection. Problem was, Ron couldn't handle waking up on time. On the morning we were due to roll, he overslept. If he'd reported for work when I did, he would have had time to ask the military CC for a rear gunner to protect our behinds. But he was sleeping while I was getting ready for work. When I realized we had a problem, I woke him up, told him that he was running late, and tried to get the military and the other trucks in the convoy to wait for us while Ron got ready. I even arranged to get a rear gun for us. But Ron didn't show up in time, and the convoy left without us. We had to wait for another convoy and escort, and—guess what—Ron didn't arrange for a rear gun this time, either.

Instead, he said he'd put himself at the end, and he'd give me his trailer to run. That was ridiculous. He was the convoy commander—we needed him up front. And by now, I wasn't so sure I wanted this guy running behind everybody. I didn't trust him—but by now I trusted myself. "Running drag is my job," I told him, "so just back off and let me do my job."

I'll be the first to admit that I was a little nervous. Still, I had to stand my ground. My assignment was to run bobtail at the end of the convoy, and I didn't want that to change just because Ron didn't want a woman back there.

So we came up with a compromise. There were a few third-country nationals driving with us who weren't with our company, so Ron decided to put two of them behind me. I was the last KBR truck in the convoy, but I had two trucks after me.

I didn't like this, but I went along with it. Ron had made a mess of things, and he definitely didn't want it on his head if something happened to me. But I didn't believe Ron for a minute when he said he would have done the same thing for a guy. I knew I could do my job, and really, so did Ron—he even said I should have been the CC on this mission.

My biggest concern, though, was security, as it always was and always would be. That's why I tried to get a rear gunner for this mission, and why I got into arguments with CCs and other bosses who didn't seem as concerned as they should be. I wasn't going to sit quietly if I thought our drivers were getting screwed because somebody didn't care or was just plain lazy.

As we were pulling out of camp, I noticed someone on the roadside counting the number of trucks leaving camp. That was never a good sign. Insurgents often had spotters who monitored our convoys and our route and used that information to set up ambushes and IEDs on the roadside.

We had been told not to allow any civilian traffic to get between us as we traveled along a narrow, two-lane road. I took this very seriously since I was running drag and we had no tail gunner to protect me. At one point, a green Mercedes pulled out into the oncoming lane and tried to pass me. I moved closer to the truck in front of me so the Mercedes couldn't sneak between us. The Mercedes stayed beside me, but when the driver saw traffic heading toward him, he tried to squeeze in ahead of me. He hit my truck and went spinning off the side of the road. We didn't stop.

The road took us through a crowded marketplace in the middle of a small town. Ron, who was riding up front, radioed back to us that things looked dangerous. The MPs who were escorting us in a separate vehicle pointed their weapons at the crowd as we started to slow down because of traffic. We were sitting ducks. If there was a suicide bomber in that crowd, that would be the end of us and lots of other people, too.

We were all supposed to turn left at a certain point. I saw the others making the turn, but as I got closer to the intersection, I could see that I was going to be trapped by oncoming traffic. The lead military escort truck had been blocking traffic so the other military vehicles could get through. Since we were not really part of the convoy, and were tucked onto the end, I knew the military would allow traffic to flow once they were through the intersection. As the last military truck completed the turn, the lead escort fell in behind—and that meant trouble. I could get separated from the convoy. And if that happened, not only was I lost, I was even more vulnerable to attack.

As traffic closed in, I had only one way out: I pulled onto the median strip, barely missing a truck, and floored it. Thank God I wasn't hauling a trailer, because I couldn't have made that move. I don't know how many people or cars I sprayed with dirt and rocks from my spinning tires as I sped down the unpaved median. It didn't matter at the moment. All I kept thinking was, *Don't get cut off. Don't let them stop you.* After about a quarter mile, I caught up with the convoy. The two trucks behind me weren't able to move as fast, and they got cut off, but nothing bad happened to them. Nobody was looking for a fight in that marketplace, at least not on this day.

I don't think that it hit me what kind of real danger I had been in till it was all over. I cried when we finally pulled into the airport. I hated crying, but I couldn't help myself. It was the first time I felt really vulnerable.

As it turned out, I got a break from the road for a while—not that I asked for it or even wanted it. When I returned to Kuwait after an uneventful trip from BIAP, a project manager asked me if I'd serve as a driver for one of the bosses. It meant driving an SUV, not a truck, and being away from the convoys. I said I'd do it, but only if it didn't become a full-time job. I wanted to stay in a truck, on the convoys, bringing supplies to the troops.

The job fell through, but before it did, the company sent my truck out with some other driver. So I was stuck working nights, loading reefers, fueling trucks and trailers, setting them up for convoy the next day, and not much else. I hated it.

With all this time on my hands, I couldn't help but think about Jack. He was due back in Kuwait soon after his R&R back home. I found myself wondering whether he was telling me the truth about his supposedly shattered marriage. A friend of mine, a convoy commander I'll call Ed, knew Jack and knew about my feelings for him. The two of us spent a lot of time together during this lull. It was good to have somebody to talk to, a guy who didn't seem like he was just trying to get me into bed.

Just after Jack went home for R&R, I had an interesting exchange with a tanker driver I'll call Bob. Several of us were talking in the lobby of the towers in Kuwait. Bob said something about Jack being away on R&R, and that he was married. "There's plenty of single guys around," he said, looking right at me. "You want to fuck?"

I was shocked. I mean, guys had come on to me, but never like this—right in front of his friends, no less. I kept my head, and said what I had told other guys (who were more subtle): "You couldn't handle the pressure."

Usually that would be the end of it. Not with Bob. He then told me in detail what he would or could do to me in bed. I walked away. But that night, I reported Bob to the night foreman, who said he'd take up the issue with his boss. They decided that Jack ought to have a "gentlemanly" talk with Bob, rather than report the incident up the chain of command.

In the middle of all this, I heard from my ex-husband Bill. He said something about quitting his job in the States and coming to Iraq to drive. That was the last thing I wanted. I knew—I knew—that I didn't want to be running into Bill on the roads of Iraq. After we spoke, I told my bosses that he was trying to get hired, and then I told them what he had done to me. I knew that would put an end to any notion of Bill driving the same roads I was.

Finally, in mid-November, I was assigned to a convoy. Jack was back, and he would be the CC on this mission.

The night before we were due to pull out, however, military intelligence got word of a plot to blow up the towers, the apartment complex where we were staying in Kuwait. This wasn't the first bomb scare we had had in the towers, but the military seemed to take this one a lot more seriously. In the past, they had brought in bomb-sniffing dogs, checked out the buildings, and then let us return. This time, we were told to evacuate and that we wouldn't be allowed back for three or four days. A little later on, we were called to a meeting and told that the towers were being evacuated permanently. We had to get all our stuff out right away. Some of the newer guys seemed worried, but a lot of us veterans weren't too concerned. We figured it was all a ploy by KBR to get out of its contract with the towers!

I didn't get a lot of sleep that night, but I was more than ready to get on the road the following morning, a Friday. We were bound for Camp Dogwood again, loaded with produce, ice, and other supplies. Part of the trip would take us along sixty miles of dirt roads, with nothing but desert on either side of us. It was one of the most dangerous roads in Iraq, not because of the insurgents, but because of the dust.

There were twenty-five of us in the convoy. Try to imagine the dust kicked up by twenty-five trucks on a dirt road. Then try to imagine what it was like when we passed a convoy going in the opposite direction. There were times when I couldn't see Jack's truck, directly in front of me. One of our drivers, Brian, collided head-on with another truck, driven by a TCN who was trying to move his rig to the front of the line. Brian was just two trucks behind me. Luckily for him, neither truck was going very fast, otherwise he'd have been killed. As it was, he was pretty banged up, enough to get sent home. Another one of our guys got hurt trying to get Brian out of his truck.

When we pulled into Dogwood on November 15, the

troops gave us a hero's welcome. Their treatment of us made all the risks and dangers seem worth it—even when we found out that they didn't really need the stuff we brought them! The camp was scheduled to be shut down in mid-December, just a few weeks later, and they pretty much had everything they'd need until then. So much for coordination.

The day after we arrived, a Sunday, the troops invited us to a volleyball game and an old-fashioned cookout. We had spent some time with them the night before, getting drunk and telling stories. It's amazing how quickly you bond with strangers in a place like this. I guess I made a few new friends, because before the volleyball game, some of the troops singled me out for a hilarious practical joke. The guys who disarm roadside bombs chased me around camp with one of their robots. It was armed with a camera and a claw, and I couldn't shake the damn thing. It followed me everywhere I went, until I escaped by climbing on top of a five-ton Army truck. I couldn't get down. Everybody was laughing so hard they had trouble catching their breath, which was fine. After all, these guys deserved a few laughs. Think about the kind of work they do, and why they need that robot.

Later, over a dinner of T-bone steaks with all the fixin's, the mood got a little more serious. Some of the troops had been with Jessica Lynch's unit that spring when it was surrounded and she was taken prisoner. Lynch, a 19-year-old supply clerk with the U.S. Army, was injured and captured by Iraqi forces after her group was ambushed on March 23, 2003, near Nasiriyah. Eleven other soldiers were killed. Lynch's famously televised rescue on April 1 was the first successful rescue of an American POW since World War II and the first ever of a female soldier. They stll felt tremendously guilty— not because she was a female, but because she was a fellow soldier and buddy—and they were second-guessing themselves. If they hadn't gotten cut off from Lynch's party, maybe things would have been different. Of course, if they hadn't gotten cut off, they might have been killed and Lynch still would have been taken prisoner. As always, I came away from my contact with our troops tremendously impressed by their courage.

Unfortunately, not everybody felt the same way I did. Some of the drivers were in it for the money alone. I saw drivers disappear when they should have been helping to unload their trucks or do a little extra to get the job done. That bothered me a lot: I just didn't understand why or how another American could have that attitude. I suppose it's always like that in war—most everybody goes above and beyond, but there are always people who are looking out just for themselves.

We were due to leave Dogwood for BIAP on Monday, the day after our volleyball game and cookout. I told Jack that I wanted to run in the last position on the convoy. He got pissed, and said that nobody else got to choose, and since I wanted to be treated like everybody else, I shouldn't make any requests, either. So I told him I'd treat him just like any other CC and I'd just go to the back of the line. And so I did.

I was pissed, and Jack was pissed. But as we pulled out, this other stuff faded into the background. Above us were a bunch of helicopters. We were going to have air support for the ride from Dogwood to the airport. That was in addition to a tail gunner who was riding behind me.

Throughout Iraq, U.S. troops and Iraqi security forces were coming under increasingly brazen attacks. Rocket fire hit the center of Baghdad in mid-November, while more than a dozen people were killed in car bomb attacks on police stations north of the capital.

We all were aware of the dangers, but truth be told, they were like a distant thunderstorm. Somebody, somewhere was getting the brunt of it—we just heard about it. But that's not to say that our trips were like driving a rig on some U.S. interstate. During one trip in late November from BIAP to Kuwait, we got stuck in a traffic circle, and while we were idling, waiting for traffic to clear, some guy exposed himself to me. It was unnerving. What if he weren't just a pervert, but a suicide bomber? What if he had a suicide belt around his waist? The next time we drove from the airport to Kuwait, I drove right behind Jack. We were all vulnerable out on the road, and maybe I seemed more vulnerable than most because of my sex. When we stopped for any reason, my truck always drew a crowd of Iraqis who just wanted a peek at an unusual sight: a female civilian truck driver.

But vulnerable or not, I was gaining more confidence in myself and in the job I was doing. I was testing myself with every mission, and, as far as I was concerned, I was meeting every challenge. I was doing my job, and then some. So I put in a request to be a convoy commander. I knew I could do it, if I got the chance.

In early December, we were prepping for another run, this one to Camp Diamondback near Mosul, about fourteen hundred kilometers from Kuwait and about thirty miles south of the border with Turkey. Another danger appeared in the desert: rain, of all things. It poured for four days. It's never fun to drive under these kinds of conditions, but in Iraq, it was extremely dangerous. There was no sealant on the roads, so when they were wet, it was like driving on a long ribbon of black ice. Hit the brakes too hard and you wind up in a wreck.

The rain brought another problem: Mud. Camp Cedar, where we often stayed overnight, was so muddy the military wouldn't let in convoys. As the assistant convoy commander—Jack was the CC—I was worried that we'd have to spend a night out on the road instead of inside the wire at Cedar.

Our first stop was Camp Tallil, an Air Force camp just a few miles from Cedar 2. Right after we pulled in, some Air Force personnel told us that our trucks had to be inspected. That meant turning around and driving back outside the camp to the inspection area, which had turned into a muddy bog. Our Army escorts were furious, but they brought us back outside the camp. Jack was asked to do a favor for the Army and pick up an ice trailer from Tallil and take it to Scania, so he drove in with the first two trucks, and both of them got stuck in the mud. Jack didn't get stuck, but as CC, he had to stay with the two drivers.

The Army had another fit and told the Air Force that the rest of us were not about to get stuck in the mud, too. We were told to stage on the road—that meant we were supposed to bring our trucks outside the camp, park them, and get our military escorts. Usually our staging area was within the camp, but because of the conditions in the camp, we staged on the road outside. With Jack preoccupied with the stuck trucks, I was now in charge. As we left the camp, one of the TCNs hit a wretch, which is a platform used to get cargo containers on and off the trailers. Our escorts said I had to stay with the driver, so I sent the rest of the convoy to a semisecure area outside the camp, called a "rom point," which served as a refueling point for military vehicles and third-country national trucks. Meanwhile I waited for help.

Our escorts left a couple of soldiers and a Humvee with a mounted gun to cover us while we waited. One of the soldiers was pretty damn nervous. We were in an unsecure area outside the wire, and he didn't like it. He drove me nuts. He kept talking about how the military had intelligence that the insurgency was moving south. Having been there a while myself, I knew that the road from Kuwait to Cedar was relatively safe. "Nothing ever happens between Cedar and Kuwait," I told him. "This is the most boring part of any mission." But he was new in country and nothing I told him would ease his anxiety.

I was getting nervous, too, but for a different reason. We were supposed to get to Camp Cedar, which was only two miles away, by nightfall. It was getting late. I called a boss at Camp Cedar, and he had a fit—everybody was having fits—and told me that it wasn't my job to stay with the TCNs. They were the Army's responsibility. My job, he said, was to get our drivers to safety before it got dark. I told him I would get it done.

Finally, the company's safety crew arrived to help the TCNs, and I rushed to the road, where the rest of the convoy was waiting. But now I had another problem: Our escorts didn't want to take us to Cedar. I had a talk with the sergeant in charge of the escort. He tried telling me that no convoys were being allowed into Cedar. I told him that my boss said that we had to be behind the wire before dark. He still refused.

"You can escort us in or we'll go without you," I told the sergeant. I reminded him that under company policy, we could ride from Tallil to Cedar without an escort. "But," I told the sergeant, "my boss would rather you escort us in." Finally, he relented and escorted us into camp. Meanwhile, Jack was still stuck in Tallil.

When we finally got to Cedar safely, I had to find somewhere to park that wasn't a bog. Then I had to arrange for an escort for the rest of the trip. At one point, one of my bosses approached me about leading the convoy the rest of the way. He asked me if I thought I could handle it.

"I handled it today," I said.

That seemed like a pretty good argument. I was looking forward to showing what I could do.

I didn't get the chance. The bosses decided not to

send us ahead with me in charge because, one of them said, "Jack would be pissed." That made me mad. I believed that if people didn't know that Jack and I were involved—and they did know—I would have gotten a chance to be a CC. In fact, one of the bosses had told me that he wouldn't put me as CC, because that would mean splitting up Jack and me. I said, "So?"

Now, because of Jack, I was being held back.

Jack finally joined us, and we left for Anaconda. It was a routine ride, but once we got there, all hell was breaking loose nearby. The night we arrived, I could hear mortar fire in the distance. The following day, twenty-two trucks in two convoys were attacked, and a couple of drivers were killed—both of them TCNs. Some of the trucks pulled into Anaconda, and the drivers showed us the bullet holes in their rigs. There was a rumor making the rounds that their military escorts, who were MPs, ran off when the shooting started. That didn't sound right, but it made me nervous. Our escorts were MPs, too. I was starting to get a bad feeling about the rest of this trip. We still had a full day of driving until we got to Mosul.

Jack wasn't making it any easier. It was pretty obvious that he was finished with me. And making matters worse, my relationship with him was costing me a chance to become a convoy commander.

My anxiety about the trip to Mosul turned out to be a

false alarm. We weren't attacked; there were no roadside bombs or ambushes along the way. I was stunned by the scenery. As we drove closer to the Turkish border, the landscape changed from flat and monotonous to mountainous and majestic. The mountains were a glorious sight, and after driving so long in the desert, they almost seemed like a mirage on the horizon.

We were in Mosul for three days while we waited to get unloaded. That gave me a chance to do some shopping in the camp stores run by local Iraqis. I loved meeting the Iraqi people and browsing through some of the really beautiful stuff they made themselves. The men who ran the shops were always respectful, which, frankly, was not what I was expecting. Women in general are not held in high regard in that part of the world, but I think the shopowners realized that they had no choice but to show respect for American women.

We left Mosul on December 8, with the breathtaking mountain scenery farther behind us with each passing mile. When we pulled into Anaconda for the night, other drivers and soldiers asked us what time we had left our base in Mosul. It seemed like an odd question, but we told them we had left at about eight o'clock. Why did that matter?

About the same time, one of our drivers came running to where we were standing. He was out of breath when he got to us. "I just heard on the radio that a suicide bomber hit the front gate of the base right after we left," he said.

When we left the gate that morning, we got stuck in traffic. Our escorts had to make us a path out. But before they did, we were just sitting there, completely vulnerable.

"Think about this," I said to one of the drivers. "That suicide bomber must have been sitting in that traffic just outside the gate when we rolled by this morning." The other driver didn't say a word. We just looked at each other—if we had been delayed just a little longer, we could have been killed or hurt in that blast.

I knew my family and friends back home knew I was in Mosul and knew I was scheduled to leave there this morning. Maybe that's one of the drawbacks of being in touch so easily with the folks back home. While it's comforting for them to hear from me, maybe at times they have too much information, and too much to worry about.

I waited in line for a phone at the camp, and finally called my father in Georgia. I didn't care about the time difference—I just wanted everybody back home to know that I was okay.

Most people back home probably wouldn't have even noticed a little news item about a suicide bomber in Mosul. The attack actually caused only minor damage, and nobody was killed or seriously hurt. But for a few people, that little news item could have created hours or days of anxiety. It bothered me that some guys hid things from their spouses and families back home. I often read postings on websites from wives who had no idea what was going on, and it was killing them with needless anxiety. I made it a point to make sure that my family knew what was happening.

I was back in Kuwait in mid-December, safe and sound and waiting for a new assignment, when we got word that our guys had found Saddam cowering in some hole in the ground. Drivers who were out on missions blew their horns when they got the news. When I saw maps on television showing the area where he had been found, I realized I had been in that neighborhood several times.

Everybody was thrilled, but we also were well aware that Saddam's loyalists might be looking for revenge. Our housing complex was placed on lockdown. I was under no illusions that everything would be fine and peaceful with Saddam out of the picture. I sent an email home to everybody, just in case they thought the days of suicide bombers and IEDs and ambushes were over, just because Saddam was in some Iraqi prison.

"I want ya'll to know that just because he has been caught doesn't mean that the violence will stop," I wrote. "We here expect it to increase for a while."

Christmas was approaching. I found myself thinking

more and more about everybody back home. I had put in for a two-week R&R in late January and planned to fly home to see as many people as I could, especially my boys. My oldest, Kenny, was getting ready to go for advanced infantry training in the summer. Hard as it was for me to believe, Kenny was nineteen years old, a young man any mother would be proud of. I couldn't wait to see him.

On the morning of Christmas Eve, we drove to Camp Cedar to pick up reefer trailers. It was a short trip, but Jack certainly made it seem longer and more difficult than it should have been. At one point he called me stupid, for reasons I don't even remember. What a generous Christmas present.

Still, I tried to be cheerful. I bought a little Christmas tree and put it in my truck. Jack and some of the other guys gave me shit about it, but I didn't care. "It doesn't matter where you are on Christmas," I told them. "We should all be celebrating. We are alive!" I tried hard to lift everybody's mood, including my own, but in the end, Jack and the other guys weren't having any Christmas cheer.

On Christmas Day, I was back in Kuwait City, by myself. I felt terribly lonely in a very lonely place. I couldn't remember being alone, really alone, on Christmas.

I was in a funk for days, partly because the work was pretty damn boring. I suppose it's like that some of the time in war zones: You wait around until the next emergency, or the next battle, and for the time being your worst enemy is boredom. I sat around with other drivers, playing cards and bitching about how bored we all were. We made a couple of runs here and there, with nothing to report except for a few rock-throwing incidents.

During this little interlude, I had a run-in with a female CC who threatened to report me for "not following instructions." This CC, in her hurry to be done for the day, left me sitting by myself in a dark area of the camp. I had insisted that someone sign the paperwork for the mail load I was hauling, releasing me from responsibility. This was going to cut into her free time, and she got pissed and left me there, alone. I know that may not sound like a big deal, since I was inside the camp, but we had all heard the rumors of female soldiers being raped in the camps, and KBR preached the buddy system. And yet there I was, left by myself, in the dark, by the CC who was responsible for my safety and security.

After sitting by myself for more than two hours, I went to the staging area to find her already in her truck and in bed. The next morning, during a briefing, she proceeded to call me down in front of the whole crew. This was more than just addressing an issue—this was outright degradation, because she harped on it for a while. I walked out in the middle of the briefing. When I got back to Kuwait, I was called into the APO office for a talk.

Yes, I was wrong for walking out on the CC's briefing.

But once I stated my side, the bosses agreed that she would not write me up and I would not write her up. But again, I stepped on some toes, and that habit would come back to haunt me.

Amid the boredom and gloom, the calendar turned to a new year, 2004, and to a date that had special meaning for me: January 7, the first "anniversary" of the day I nearly died at the hands of my ex-husband. My mental state wasn't good, and neither was my physical state. I was coughing my toenails up, and I had a wicked sore throat.

In the middle of all this, I split up with Jack. For a while, I had been plotting to get us sent to different locations. When Jack was sent to another camp, I intervened with the bosses and asked to be sent to a theater distribution center, or TDC, in Kuwait. A TDC is a place where supplies are stored and then shipped to various camps. It was the only time that I let my personal life rule what I was doing in my job, but I knew that if Jack and I were working out of the same place, it would not end. I got my wish, and then I got ready for my first trip back home.

THREE

IT DID MY HEART GOOD TO SEE my boys. All three of them were becoming such fine young men. My oldest, Kenny, was thinking all the things young people think about at his age: What was he going to be? Where was his place in the world? He joined the National Guard and was thinking about auditioning for a spot in the National Guard Band in Little Rock.

I flew into Memphis on January 20, rented an SUV, and drove to my mom's house in DeWitt. I spent the night there and then drove to Memphis to see the boys the following morning. During the drive, I heard on the radio that the group 3 Doors Down was playing in Memphis the following night. Once I got my hotel room, I got on the computer and bought four tickets for the show. We'd have a great old time together.

I got sick soon after I arrived in Memphis, so my reunion with the boys wasn't exactly what I would have liked. They went to the movies that night without me. But I was well enough to go to the concert with them, and just as I imagined, we had a blast. Ian, my middle boy, and I watched from our seats because he didn't want to be part of the mosh pit, but Kenny and Steffan dove right in. I watched as Kenny floated across the top of people's heads, being handed from one person to another. I laughed. The boys had grown some. Being the ages that they were at that time, they were doing the growth spurt thing. We had great fun. They didn't really ask me too much about Iraq and I didn't tell them much. That was fine with me.

I ate home cookin' for two weeks, and it was great—just what I needed. I caught up with friends and family, especially Mamaw. I hadn't seen her since Papaw's death. I showed her the heart-shaped rock I found on the other side of the world on the day Papaw was buried. I wanted her to have it, but she insisted that I keep it.

And, believe it or not, I saw Bill.

He and I had been exchanging emails while I was in Kuwait and Iraq, and even though I felt myself finally moving away from him, I also wanted to see him. I suppose I wanted to see if he had changed, like he said he would. I drove to Arcadia, Kansas, to see him and his mother, Carole. I had planned to stay for a couple of days, but it didn't take long for me to wish that I had stayed away. He was the same old Bill—not the Bill I had fallen in love with, but the other Bill, the Bill who nearly killed me, and now seemed intent on killing himself. I could only pity him.

Spending time with Bill reminded me of how much I had changed and grown in the last few months. I realized that I didn't want to live the kind of life I had been living when we were married.

Afterward, I summed it up in my journal: "I don't want to just survive my life. I want to really live it."

I landed back in Kuwait City on February 3 at 11:20 P.M. and reported for work at three o'clock that morning. Not exactly a whole lot of time to get adjusted to reality (never mind sleep), but things were changing at headquarters, and I was a part of those changes.

I left Kuwait as a driver, but I returned as a lead person at the TDC. The company needed somebody to get the convoys organized and moving every morning. The job meant doing lots of paperwork and setting up assignments for the following morning. I had done some of that work before I left for R&R, when I had a bad cold. My foreman had said I was too sick to drive, but I couldn't just sit around waiting to get better. So I worked in the yard, doing reports and setting up that day's convoy. I guess that whoever noticed liked the way I did the job. Now our foreman was getting ready to leave, and our lead man—the person who usually does the job I did while I was sick—was being groomed to move up to foreman. So I became the lead person.

The promotion was nice, but all I ever wanted to be was a convoy commander. Only one other woman I knew of had been made a CC, and I wanted to be the next one. Besides, I came to Iraq to help the troops, and every time I pulled into a camp with ice or whatever I was hauling, I felt like I was doing exactly that. The troops were always so happy and grateful to see us rolling in. That made it all worthwhile.

Working in the yard meant that I would no longer go out on missions. I'd miss the work and the experience of meeting the troops, but the truth of the matter was that the missions themselves were changing. No more reefers were going out. My company, KBR, no longer had a contract to handle food, and, in any case, it was winter, so ice wasn't in big demand. The TCNs were given the job of hauling whatever ice was necessary.

The alternative, driving flatbeds, didn't appeal to me. Flatbed drivers didn't come into contact with the troops very often. And besides, I was trying to keep away from Jack, and working the yard would achieve that goal.

Part of the new job's excitement was my lack of preparation and training—they just threw me into the job without a whole lot of guidance. I was the person getting the convoys out of the yard in the morning, a pretty important task. I could get the paperwork done and have a convoy ready to roll out about an hour and a half quicker than they had before.

I did think about what I was doing: I was the person sending these convoys out on their missions, and some of those missions were dangerous. The missions at that moment were from Kuwait to Camp Cedar, a safe run. But I knew that pretty soon I could be sending them to places like Anaconda, where it was really getting hot. Convoys were getting hit, which was not that unusual, but they also weren't getting the protection at the border from the military that they deserved. Some of the military guys didn't seem to give a shit, because they were due to go home soon. That attitude was going to kill or hurt some driver.

My boss and I started asking some of the contractors to write up reports about what was going on at the border—convoys getting rocked, and worse. We took those reports to the company's safety office. It just so happened that one of the company's safety bigwigs from Houston had dropped by for a firsthand look at things in Kuwait. We let him have it. We told him that the job was more dangerous than ever, and our people needed more protection.

The guy from Houston seemed surprised to hear this. He asked if he could talk in person to some of the drivers, so my foreman and I set up a meeting with some of the guys who had been on the latest convoy that got hit. My boss and I left the room when everybody was in place. We didn't want the Houston guy to think this was some kind of setup or that we were coaching the guys.

The next morning, I handed in seventeen reports

from drivers who had complaints about getting rocked at the border and the military not doing anything about it. Rocks aren't as dangerous as bullets, but they could seriously hurt or even kill a driver if they were heavy enough to smash through a windshield. Some of the drivers said they saw Humvees nearby, with troops fooling around with Iraqi kids, while they were getting rocked. To his credit, the safety officer sat down with me and some of the guys during lunch in the dining facility. The guys told the officer exactly what they thought of the company's safety policy.

In the middle of this, some other bigwig came by and asked me what everybody was talking about. I had the guys repeat some of their stories, and I added a few choice opinions of my own.

In the short term, I think I did some good by not keeping my mouth shut. In the following days, our convoys made it safely back into Kuwait without being rocked or being forced to leave the roadway to avoid dangerous obstacles. But we weren't about to fool ourselves—we knew it was a matter of time before it started up again. And when it did, we'd make a fuss again. I didn't care how many times I had to open my mouth and let the bigwigs know the truth. If that's what it takes to get the military to do its job, I said, then I'll be a nuisance. I'd do whatever it took to protect my guys.

Before I knew it, I was doing it all by myself. My boss

simply stopped coming to work. He was on a drinking binge. He and I were friends and we rode into work together. I went to see him each day to catch him up on what was going on and he was drunk every time I saw him. Once he made the mistake of coming to dinner one night while he was drunk and other people saw him that way. One of those people reported him to someone and they fired him. That was bad enough, but the other guy who was helping out in the office was on R&R, which left me to do all the paperwork and convoy preparation by myself for a couple of days. I ran around like a chicken without a head, but I managed to keep everything moving.

In late February, I got a respite from the yard. I was assigned to a convoy to get a firsthand look at the safety problems I had been complaining about to the bosses. There was talk that we might have to drive as far north as Anaconda, which is a little north of Baghdad. The CC was was my friend Ed, who had a reputation as an aggressive commander. Ed and I had worked together before and had become pretty good friends. He was an experienced CC, which was good, because many of the drivers on this convoy had never driven this far north. I knew I'd bring some extra experience to the convoy, since I had been to Anaconda before.

Just before we left, we got word that a driver named Al Cayton had been killed when an IED exploded on a highway in northern Iraq. He was on his way to Kuwait for R&R.

Al was sixty years old. He came over to Iraq in June 2003, after the company he drove for, Consolidated Freightways, went belly up. He had worked for CF for thirty-two years and had logged three million miles without an accident. Because of that unbelievable record, he was a member of a group called "America's Road Team," a collection of the country's safest truck drivers. These drivers don't just drive; they go to schools and other public venues to talk about the importance of highway safety.

Al was not only a damn good driver—he was a true patriot. After September 11, he was part of a convoy that drove some remains of the World Trade Center around the country, so people outside of the New York area could see what the terrorists did to us. Al left behind a wife, a daughter, and two sons.

Two other drivers in Al's convoy were seriously wounded in the attack. The news of Al's death made getting back in a truck a little scarier, but it also reminded me of why I was so obsessed with safety. We had to do everything we could to protect our drivers, because if we didn't, we would lose people. It was that simple.

In the end we didn't have to go to Anaconda after all, which was a relief. We weren't rocked or ambushed on the trip, which was good, but even better were some of the changes I noticed on our way. On past trips I had seen the bombed-out hulks of cars along the road—the roadside looked like a junkyard. But now they were gone. The land was being cleared of the reminders of war, and the people were getting on with their lives.

When I got back to Kuwait, I found myself in the middle of a power struggle over who was going to be the new foreman (it wasn't going to be me). It reminded me of why I wanted to get back out on the road. I had no time for all this crap.

I told one of my supervisors that a guy who was going to be made a CC had no business leading a convoy. I already had told some of the midlevel guys the same thing, and when they didn't listen, I went over their heads. I had seen this guy blatantly disobey his CC on another mission, and I knew that he refused to wear his flak jacket and helmet, which was a violation of company rules. That didn't bother me so much, because we all took off our helmets once we were out of sight of safety officers. But it was his attitude—he made a show of not wearing his helmet, which could have gotten his CC in trouble. How can you lead if you're not willing to follow?

The supervisor paid more attention to me than the midlevel guys did. In fact, the supervisor said he wanted to meet with this would-be CC right away. When one of those midlevel guys who ignored my complaints got wind of what was going on, he found the guy I complained about and personally brought him to the supervisor. The guy basically admitted to everything I complained about. So he not only got crossed off the CC list, he was pulled out of the TDC yard and sent to the maintenance yard, where they could keep an eye on him. There was talk about giving him a one-way ticket home.

And I was given a ticket to the overnight shift. I didn't think that was a coincidence, but I didn't care. All I cared about was the drivers. In the middle of all this, we lost another driver—one of the guys who was hurt in that ambush a week or so earlier died of his wounds. The body count for our company, KBR, was now more than forty.

My website continued to generate lots of emails from people in the States who heard about it through friends and relatives. My sister Mary kept it updated by posting my emails home along with pictures I took with my digital camera. Because I had so many requests for my email, I had a very long contact list. Eventually, Yahoo stopped me from sending out all these emails because they classified them as bulk mail. So I formed a Yahoo group, which allowed registered viewers to read my emails and post their responses.

Sometimes I'd get emails from people who were either thinking of coming to Iraq as contractors, or who knew or loved somebody who was thinking about it. I encouraged people to get in touch with me and promised that I'd give them the truth. I was willing to answer any question, at any time. On March 1, I received this email from the States from a young woman whose boyfriend was thinking of applying for a job with Halliburton. She had heard about my website from a friend.

Understandably she was nervous about her boyfriend. She asked me if I considered it safe in Iraq. Would I recommend my job to anyone?

Here's my response, which I sent by email and which Mary posted on the site.

I am not sure that I can answer your
question in the manner that you wish.
Some people like me have seen very little
of the really bad stuff and others have
been shot at and taken mortar fire. The

closest mortar fire I have seen was at Mosul back in December. One landed about 150 yards from the truck I was sleeping in. It rocked my truck and I came out looking to see if it hit anything. Friends of mine have had mortars bounce off their tanker trucks. I have had rocks thrown at my truck and some hit and some miss. I had some friends that were here when the war was going on get bricks in their windshields and go home because of it. I have been stopped in the middle of the road just south of Baghdad for a couple of hours because the Army found an IED and had the road blocked while they cleared it. But just this last week we lost 2 drivers and have 2 still in the hospital because the SUV that they were driving was hit by an IED.

Now don't let all this overwhelm you. I don't know where you live, but find the newspaper to the biggest town near you and look and see how many people were killed in that city just overnight. I am not sure what the death toll for the military is to date. I do not watch the news. It is biased and only reports the bad that is going on. It doesn't report the good—like Sgt. Maples, who I met out in Dogwood, who helped rebuild a school, and how grateful the people were.

I don't look at it as whether it is safe or unsafe. We are doing good work here. Yes, some of us won't be coming home when all is said and done. But for me it is more than the money that brings me here. There is no amount of money that can be paid for me to risk my life. But there is good to be done in this world and if we as individuals wait for someone else to do it, it will never get done.

My best wishes to you and your boyfriend. Please, let me know if he decides to come on over. I would love to meet him.

I will say a prayer for the 2 of you as you make this decision.

The young woman's boyfriend, Rodney, eventually decided to come over, and although I never met him, I did meet a friend of his. He told me that he had read my response to to Rodney's girlfriend, and because of that, he decided to come to Iraq as well.

It was two o'clock in the morning on the night of March 9. I was asleep in my room in the Safir, a resort in Kuwait where KBR housed a lot of its contractors.

Somebody else was in the room. I didn't hear him come in, but I knew he was there. He was holding a knife at my throat. He told me to keep my mouth shut.

What happened next wasn't really happening to me. It was happening to somebody else. I was just watching. *She realizes in an instant why he was in the room, why he had a knife, what he wanted. "Don't make a sound," he is saying. "Not even a whimper. If you do, I'll slit your throat and fuck you until the last drop of blood drips from your body."*

She feels his fingers stab into her. She is biting her lip, trying not to scream. But shouldn't she? Does she want to live through this? Does it matter if he kills her? What about the other women in the building? If she screams and they hear her and try to help her, will he kill them, too?

She feels terrible pain. The knife is pressing harder, and so is he. He stops for a moment, looks up, and sees a picture of three boys taped to the headboard of her bed. "I'm sure your boys would like to see their mom again," he says. "Another sound out of you and they will, but in a box."

When did she make any noise? She didn't make a sound, or did she? She shakes her head—"No! Don't kill me!"—and as she does, she can feel a sting as the knife cuts her slightly.

The boys! That's it. She'll think about them, concentrate on them. She will get through this so she can see them again.

"Oh, God, he is hurting me!" She screams, but it is a silent scream.

She is with her boys in a playground near her mom's house. She can hear her youngest boy telling her that she's the best mom in the world. The two of them are hanging upside down on the monkey bars.

He grabs her hair and jerks her head. What did she do? She didn't make a sound.

She asks her son why he said that.

Another sharp, awful pain.

"Because you know how to be a kid," her son says. "And how to have fun."

He tells her that she is good, nice and tight.

She laughs and tells her boy that she has the three best sons in the world.

He tells her that if she's lucky, he'll visit her again in the future.

Her son smiles and laughs as they swing on the bars with the blood rushing to their heads.

He's going to come back and do this to her again? She knows she couldn't live through that.

They race each other to the swings to see who can swing higher.

Another stabbing pain. Get it over with, she is thinking. Just don't kill me. Even though she thinks he is killing something inside her.

The boys are older now. It is Christmas. The oldest boy is telling her about the girls who say he's a good dancer. They want to know where he learned to dance so well.

How long is he going to torture her? How much more can she take?

"I told them I learned to dance from my mom," the boy says. "The girls think that's so sweet." His mom can feel tears rolling down her cheeks.

Did she make a noise? She thought she heard something. He didn't seem to notice. How did that nightgown get above her breast? She doesn't remember him lifting it up that far.

She asks her boy if he wants to dance. They look at each other and smile.

Another sharp pain, but this one in the chest. She whimpers as he bites down hard on her nipple.

The boys run into the living room and clear away the furniture.

She is trying not to scream, but it hurts. It feels like he is trying to bite off her nipple.

The oldest boy cranks up the stereo. First, a bit of rock and roll.

He is whispering in her ear again, but she can't make out the words.

They jam to the music, and then find some oldies. She and her boy take to the floor and do the fox-trot.

Again, he whispers in her ear, but this time she can hear what he's saying. "Get up. Come on and get the fuck up." He leads her to the bathroom, with the knife at her back. He shuts the door and locks it behind them. He tells her to turn on the water as hot as it will go. She is paralyzed. She can't do it. He grabs her hair and puts the knife to her throat and turns on the shower. It doesn't take long before the water is scalding, burning her skin. She wants to scream.

The two other boys are laughing as their brother and their mom do the fox-trot.

"Scrub harder, all over your body," he tells her. Her body feels numb. He starts to scrub her, and doesn't even flinch when he comes in contact with the scalding water. He scrubs so hard it feels like he is peeling off her skin. He scrubs down between her legs. God, it hurts.

When he is satisfied that she is clean enough, he tells her to stay in the shower until he is gone. "You were a good girl. I liked it," he says. "Now, don't move and don't turn off the water until I'm gone. If you tell anyone about this, I'll come back and you won't be so lucky. You've given me so much pleasure and I would hate to have to kill you." He opens the bathroom door and leaves. She turns off the water, sits down, and cries. She'll never remember how long she stayed there, crying. She will never remember when she finally went back to bed. But when she wakes up after this horrible night, her body is bruised and sore.

She tries to call in sick. They tell her she has to come to work, *because they are short-handed. She gets up, takes a shower, puts on her clothes, and catches a bus to take her to the yard, just like nothing ever happened.*

She can't allow this to take over her mind. She can't tell anyone, because she doesn't want him to come back.

I had to get back on the road. I had to get away from Safir, from my room, from anything that reminded me of what happened. I felt my room was more dangerous than the roads in Iraq. I thought I recognized my attacker—I was pretty sure I had seen him somewhere. He was about six feet tall, with sandy blond hair cut in military style. He had a round face and a big nose, and his hands were really rough.

I put in a request to go back to driving reefers. I knew this would upset my family, but I also knew I couldn't tell them the real reason why. In an email home on March 4, I blamed it all on office politics, which wasn't entirely untrue:

I am going back to reefers. This was
my choice, As ya'll know, the last few

weeks have been very stressful for me. I
did put in for the foreman's position, but
pulled my resume out of the stack
tonight. I knew a long time ago that
there were a lot of politics and butt kiss-
ing going on to get some promotions
around here. And as ya'll know, I don't
play that game. Yes, to some extent I
wanted the job. But I wanted it because I
care about the drivers out at TDC. Well, I
have come to the conclusion that maybe
I care too much to be of any good to
them. I have stepped on a few toes in
what little I have done. I was told yester-
day that the drivers' concerns were not
my business.

That really burned me—the drivers' concerns
weren't my business. I had to get out of there. And after
my family read this email, I knew they'd understand why.
But still, this wasn't the whole story. And even though I
didn't want them to know what had happened, I found
myself writing the following sentence:

We have some great men and
women serving our country, but sometimes women get raped and killed on post.

Of course, nobody suspected that I knew about this first-hand.

Kenny, my oldest boy, sent back an email that meant so much to me. "I understand what you are doing," he wrote. "Just be careful and watch your ass. I love you."

I kept sending cheerful emails home, keeping every-body posted on where my new assignment might take me. It seemed for a while that I might get moved north up near Turkey, or to a camp near the border with Jordan. I said that I would have to go to Camp Anaconda for more training—I didn't mention that the camp was taking mortar or rocket fire every day.

Although it was early March, the days were getting hot in Iraq. While I waited to go back on the road, the temper-ature hit a hundred degrees. I slept outside on a balcony on my cot. I told everybody I was just trying to get used to the heat before I hit the road, but I also couldn't stand being in that bed. The sunrises were spectacular, I wrote.

All the while, I was choking on my secret.

Eventually I had to tell somebody, or I'd go crazy try-ing to pretend that nothing had happened. One day I ran into my old friend from home, Keith. He told me I looked like shit and that I was acting funny. I looked away and said something about working too hard, but he knew me well enough to know I was lying. He asked if some-thing was wrong—and he wouldn't take no for an answer. Finally I broke down and told him about the attack. Visibly angry, he told me he'd "take care of this" for me. I didn't say anything more.

My friend Ed Lawson, who was the CC during my short mission in early February, seemed different from most of the guys I met in Iraq and Kuwait. He and I became buddies while I was seeing Jack. We often had dinner together and occasionally went shopping together in Faha-heel, a little market town near our quarters in Kuwait. Most of all, we talked a lot. He told me about his marriage, that he was afraid that if he left his wife, she would go back overseas, where she was born, and take their son with him.

One night, about three weeks after the attack, I had my first chance to talk to Ed about what had happened. We had some drinks, even though alcohol is forbidden in Kuwait. I never got the chance to tell him—I got drunk, and we wound up spending the night together. It wasn't planned, and I think both of us were surprised the next morning.

Soon afterward, I told Ed about the rape. He was furious, and he insisted that I should report it. I didn't want to—because I was ashamed, but also because I didn't want to be sent home. "But you don't want this guy attacking other women," he said.

Ed got on his computer and ran through a database that had the names of servicemen in the area. Eighty-three names met my partial description. Together we tried to whittle that number down. Ed and Keith, who also was trying to identify the attacker, were my avenging angels, although neither knew the other.

Ed and I grew closer. Ed checked on me at night while he was working. If I had a problem, he said, I could call him at any time.

On April 14, I had a problem.

It was a Wednesday night. I had spent a few hours with some friends who had formed a music group that got together once a week to sing and play. When I got home, I spent some time on my computer, and then headed upstairs for bed at about eleven thirty.

He was in my room, behind the door, when I got there. Because of where I had some footlockers, I could not open my bedroom door all the way. There was a gap behind the door—that's where he was standing. As I turned to close the door, he grabbed me from behind and put his hand over my mouth. "I know what you're doing," he whispered. He told me to stop. If I kept talking, he'd come back. "It won't be an easy death," he said. Then he ran his hands across my chest and grabbed me between the legs. I told him I would scream. He gave me a look, as if to say, "Go ahead, I'll kill you." I knew that's what he was thinking. "You may kill me but they will catch you before you get out of here," I said. I think he saw in my eyes that I meant it, or maybe he realized that I didn't care whether or not he killed me. As it was, I couldn't sleep unless Ed was there to watch over me. I wasn't eating. I was hiding from the world in my villa. I didn't hang out with the guys anymore. Everyone knew something was wrong.

For whatever reason, he left.

I called Ed right away. He said he'd make a call to get some Marines to Safir right away, but I wouldn't let him. I didn't want a big scene. I told him I would report everything the following morning. But I didn't, not really. I told Ken, one of my foremen, that an intruder had gotten into my room. I didn't tell him anything more than that. He told me to give him a name and that he and some other guys would take care of this themselves. I told him I just wanted to feel safe again.

The following morning, following Ken's advice, I went to the KBR security office to report the incident. I didn't say anything about the violation—I just couldn't bring myself to talk about it. I simply said that I had found an intruder in my room the previous evening, and I asked security for a key to my room, so I could keep it locked.

Three days went by, and I didn't have a key. Coincidentally, the head of KBR security for the entire Middle East was on site. I took him aside, told him what happened, and said that nothing seemed to be happening as a result of my complaint. He gave me his card, followed up with a phone call, and eventually I emailed him a statement with the whole story about the rape and the return visit.

I left Safir for a few days to meet with the head of human resources, but when I returned, I couldn't go back to the room where it all happened. I asked to be moved, and the bosses agreed. But they asked me not to tell the other women in the complex about the attack. But by now, enough people knew that something had happened, and rumors were flying. I wound up telling other women that there was a rapist on the loose and they ought to take precautions, like getting a key for their rooms. I asked them not to mention that I told them what had happened.

KBR continued to investigate the crime, but the red tape was unbelievable. The attack took place on Kuwaiti soil, so the company and the military advised me to report it to the Kuwaiti authorities. So I had to give a statement to the Kuwaitis.

Through all of this, Ed was my rock. He was kind and understanding—I don't know if I could have made it through without his help and concern.

The day after I reported the rape to KBR, I joined Ed

for a ride to a personnel processing area near the Kuwait Airport, where all the troops and most of the contractors were processed before beginning their duties. Ed had a desk job there, and that evening I went with him to the office. While I was sitting there, Oliver North walked into the room. Several other people were gathered around him, and Ed asked me if I wanted to meet him. I said no, although I did want to—but I didn't want to bother him.

A few minutes later, Ed took me over to have my picture taken with Colonel North. He asked me what I did and thanked me for supporting the troops. That picked up my spirits.

But even still, I was thinking about going home. I told Ed how I felt.

He looked at me and said, "Are you going to let this man dictate to you what you're going to do with your life, like you have with so many others?"

"This is different," I said.

Ed was unconvinced. "What he did to you is different in a way, but the outcome will be the same. Once again, a man will stop you from doing what you want to do. Are you going to let him win?"

So I didn't go home. I went back out on the road, in Iraq, where I could feel safe.

FOUR

I WAS ROCKED ON MY FIRST mission after getting out of the office. It did nothing to change my opinion that I was safer on the road than I was in my apartment in Kuwait. I'll be honest with you: Getting rocked was exciting. It meant I was back doing what I loved to do. I was back on the road.

It was like coming home, getting back into reefers and seeing some of the guys I hadn't seen in a while. Most were glad to see me back in reefers, and they welcomed me with open arms. But not everybody was familiar. I saw a lot of new faces when our convoy got put together. Their inexperience was a nice match for our trucks—they were all new, too.

The rocking incident took place while I was driving bobtail in a convoy headed for Anaconda in the north. We were about twenty or thirty kilometers north of the Kuwait-Iraq border when it happened, along a boring part of the run from the border to Cedar. We saw some kids standing on the side of the road in the center median. One of the guys I was running with had warned us about kids throwing rocks in this area. Then, suddenly, there it was—I heard a loud crack. I never saw who threw it, but whoever it was had pretty good aim, or just got lucky. The rock cracked my windshield—my brand-new windshield. Luckily, I could still see through it.

I radioed my CC, a guy named Shane, and told him what happened. Just to tease the new guys in the convoy, who I knew were listening to the radio, I asked Shane, "Can you ask the escorts if we can turn around and do that again? They didn't get my windshield very good." The other guys had plenty to say about that. "Are you nuts?" one of them said. Another guy who probably real-ized I was kidding said, "Yes, let's do it." I heard a lot of laughs over the radio, and I had to laugh, too. "Well," I said, "I can tell I'm back in reefers. I was rocked on my first mission, and now I get rocked on my first mission back. I feel right welcome now." The incident and the way I reacted to it actually helped relax everybody, partic-ularly the new guys.

We had some TCNs in the convoy, and knowing their reputation for not keeping pace, I helped our military es-corts keep them in line. After we got to Cedar to refuel, a couple of the escorts blew kisses to me from their Humvee to say thanks.

Then it was on to Anaconda. We spent two days there, one with our trucks in the shop for routine main-tenance, and the second getting ready for a return trip south. As we prepared to head back south, one of our foremen, a guy named Ray, gave me the news I'd been waiting to hear: I would be the CC on the return trip.

I was nervous because company policy dictated that on my first few missions, an experienced CC would ride along in my convoy. In this case, the CC was Jack. Even though we had split up, we crossed paths on occasion and he still was trying to get me into bed. I wasn't going to sleep with him, but I also had to make sure I didn't piss him off—he had to evaluate me, and I wanted a good and fair evaluation.

But there was more to worry about. Things were getting hot just outside the gates on the day we were due to roll. Word spread through the camp that a little Iraqi girl had been run over by a truck, and some insurgents were looking for revenge. They fired mortars that landed near the gates, and we heard some small-arms fire. We couldn't see what was going on from our staging area, but we heard explosions, and we heard the sirens that went off when the camp was put under red alert. A voice on our radios told us to get into a bunker, although the drivers just took cover in their trucks. We'd also have to put on our personal protection gear—a helmet and body armor. That was a pain. To be honest, a few mortars didn't really bother us.

Periodically throughout the day, the gates were shut and nobody moved in or out. I couldn't help but think that this was not the way to start my first mission as a CC.

Even with the attacks, we got ready to roll. We had eight trucks in the convoy, but I also was told to take six drivers to BIAP before heading to Scania, Cedar, and finally to Kuwait. It was going to be a long haul. Just as we were getting ready to roll from the staging area, a convoy that had just left the camp came under attack. They were far enough away—about twenty kilometers—that we didn't hear any explosions, but our military escorts got on the radio and told us that we had to stop. A sergeant approached my truck and told me what was going on—

he wanted to tell me in person, he said, rather than over the radio. He didn't want to alarm the rest of the convoy. It was up to me to tell my guys.

And that was my policy—I always told my guys what I knew. Unlike some other CCs, I thought my drivers ought to know as much as I did on security matters. I think that's why so many drivers told me that they liked running in my convoys. They knew what was going on, and they could prepare themselves.

It turned out that one of our KBR personnel was severely wounded in the attack, and several others suffered minor injuries. The guys in the office were in radio contact with the convoy as the attack was going on. Later, one of the guys told me how helpless he felt listening to the drivers talking to each other during the ambush. "It's really bad," he said, "when you know you're their foreman, and you were the guy who sent them out there."

After about twenty minutes of waiting at the gate, our escorts from the Twenty-first Airborne Military Police said we were ready to proceed. "We're going to get out of here as fast as we can," one of the escorts told me. "Or else we're going to get stuck here for the night." As usual, the escorts consisted of three Humvees, each one carrying three soldiers. One Humvee rode up front, another in the middle of the convoy, and the third protected our rear. The gate opened, and out we rolled.

It was a very slow ride. As the CC, I was driving the lead truck, trying to keep my eyes on the road and on the roadside at the same time. Some of the third-country nationals in the convoy, who were essentially tagging along, were not keeping pace with the rest of us. Because they didn't speak English, we couldn't communicate with them to get them to pick up the pace—they were at the rear of the convoy. We got stuck in a traffic jam, and the TCNs did nothing to keep civilian cars out of the convoy, which made things move even slower.

After a drive that took way too long, we got to BIAP, dropped off our riders, and headed for Kuwait by way of Camp Scania and Camp Cedar. On the road from Cedar to Kuwait, one of my drivers got rocked along the same stretch of road where I was rocked on the trip north. The driver wasn't hurt, but I was pissed off that this could happen again. I radioed our military escorts, and the tail gunners said they would take care of it. One of the escorts reported back to me: "Those kids won't be rocking any more trucks for a while." I wondered what that meant. After we reached the checkpoint at the border, I asked one of the MPs what they did to the kids.

"Let's hope that they were able to walk home," the MP said.

I got the impression that the tail gunner tanned

their hides real good, and that satisfied me, because I was tired of having to replace windshields, which I did frequently, and of seeing friends of mine get glass in their eyes.

Our escorts were a great group of guys who did right by us. When I was working in the yards, I heard stories about some guys who weren't getting the job done protecting our drivers, but these guys were terrific. I had no complaints. I took their picture and emailed it home, and Mary posted it on the website.

Ed was working at the airport in Kuwait, but I heard from him constantly by email. He understood that I still was recovering from the attack—that I would always be recovering from the attack—so he was very supportive and protective at a time when I needed support and protection.

He was clear, too, that he respected me as a colleague, as a person who did her job and did it well. In one email he wrote: "As for your ability to lead a convoy, I have no doubts in your capabilities." And he had some pretty good advice, too. "Most of all," he wrote, "remember that looking like you have all the answers is almost as good as having all the answers." That certainly was true. If you look like you have all the answers, people will rally around you. Looking confident is just as important as being confident. Eventually, Ed decided on a word for our relationship. He emailed me:

> I think I have found the word and/or definition for you and I'm gonna run it by you. Some folks might not understand it . . . but here it goes. I think "arrange-ment" sounds good. I know it may sound ugly, but I looked it up and pondered on it for a while and what I picture and how I see it, it fits. The first definition is an agreement between two persons . . . The second was, "put in a purposeful way to create." So, when I pictured it in my head, I came up with a floral arrange-ment. It's beautiful and it's there. You can admire it for what it is and know there is nothing you can do to screw it up . . . I can't be honest right now and say how it will all work out, but I'm here, when and if you want, no strings attached and no promises.

As Ed phrased it, "arrangement" sounded nicer than it should have. I went along with it. It wasn't long before Ed and I were starting to plan a vacation together.

In late March 2004, four American civilians working for Blackwater Safety USA, a contracting firm, were ambushed near Fallujah. It was enough that the terrorists killed all four. After the attack, a mob rushed the cars, set them on fire, dragged the burned bodies from their SUVs, and mutilated them. They tied two bodies to the back of a car and dragged them around Fallujah. Even children got in on the act, hacking away at the bodies. Two charred corpses, or what was left of them, were strung up on a bridge over the Euphrates River. An Iraqi civilian put up a sign that read: "Fallujah is the cemetery for Americans."

Spring 2004 was a bloody time in Iraq. Five U.S. soldiers were killed the same day as those contractors. It was all part of a vicious campaign by the insurgents to stop the handover of sovereignty to the new Iraqi government.

Our military estimated that there were more than two dozen attacks a day against coalition troops.

Just after these awful murders, I got word that I would be the CC on a convoy from Anaconda to Al Asad, a camp that was west of Anaconda. This time I wouldn't have another CC in the convoy to help out. I was on my own.

I had never been to Al Asad, so the roads would be unfamiliar. And given all the attacks on convoys, I wasn't sure until the last minute whether we'd be allowed to go.

I was nervous, of course, but I buried myself in the details of the assignment, hoping that work wouldn't leave room for anxiety. One of the projected routes between Anaconda and Al Asad was near the site where the soldiers and contractors had been killed. That certainly added to everybody's sense of concern.

On the morning we were due to pull out, I attended a security briefing at six o'clock. These meetings were pretty regular, and I was one of the few faithful attendees, even though all CCs were required to attend. I asked the security officers about the ambush of the Blackwater contractors, and how that might affect my mission. The security guys pulled up reports from the Internet and showed me pictures of the aftermath of those attacks, when the terrorists defiled the corpses of their victims. The pictures were gruesome. I've never forgotten those awful images.

The reports indicated that some of the routes we might take were considered very dangerous, but I wouldn't find out which route we would follow until our military escorts arrived. After the briefing, I went to the staging lanes and met with my guys. I told them what I had read and seen. They had questions that I could not answer, so I turned to two of the guys who were familiar with the drive to Al Asad. They warned us about a town north of Anaconda where we would be slowing down to make a left turn. They also told us about a long, lonely stretch of road along the Tigris River where several convoys had come under attack from boats in the river. That was a new one for most of us.

When the escorts arrived, they told us the route—it was a dangerous one, but not as dangerous as some others. The roads we'd be taking were coded amber as opposed to red or black. Just like Homeland Security had color-coded threat levels back home, the military had color codes for threat assessments on Iraq's roads. Code Amber meant that there were minor hostilities in the area, not enough to scrap a mission. Code Red meant major hostilities, with roads closed to civilian convoys. Code Black meant that all hell was breaking loose and nobody was allowed on the road.

I sent an email home, asking everybody to pray for us. I promised to either send an email or call my father via satellite phone to let everybody know when I arrived in camp safely. For security reasons, I never mentioned the name of the camp.

We were delayed a bit, waiting for our escorts from the 660th Transportation Company, but the wait was worth it. They were a great bunch of guys and real pros. Best of all, they didn't have to fire a shot during the trip to Al Asad. It turned out to be a great ride. Most of Iraq is desert, an endless brown landscape. But on this trip, we followed a riverbed on our right. There, it was green and beautiful. To our left, there was nothing but sand. I couldn't help but marvel at the contrast—these two landscapes had no business being that close to each other.

As we approached the camp, our beautiful ride was interrupted by a sudden sandstorm. The wind was kicking up, and even with our trailers loaded down with ice, we could feel the blasts of wind hitting us. But we got behind the gates before the storm made visibility impossible.

We ran into our escorts again in the mess hall and shared a nice dinner with them. One of them said, "That was the best convoy we've been on since we got here two months ago. We'll be your escort any place at any time. If you need escorts, come find us, we will do it." I couldn't have asked for a better compliment for my first solo mission as a CC. Until this moment, I believed I could do this job. Now I knew it for sure.

It started raining before we had a chance to eat dinner. Bear in mind, this is not the kind of rain we have back in the States. This wasn't water coming down from the clouds and getting us wet. We were getting pelted with mud. The rain and the sandstorm had crossed paths, and the result was a mess. It was weird to feel the wet of the water and then look at clothes and see spots of mud.

I was standing outside the mess hall with Richard, one of my drivers, and some of our escorts when we heard an explosion in the distance. Nobody in the mess hall moved. It seemed pretty routine. About twenty minutes later, we were told to clear the building immediately. My escorts—the guys with the guns—took off in the direction of one of their vehicles. Richard and I ran with the escorts to their five-ton truck. All the while, I was on the radio with my guys, letting them know what was going on. Somebody asked if I was serious.

The troops helped us get in the back of their truck, which was no easy task. The truck was pretty big, and we had to climb up to get in. The troops gave us their helmets and started to give us their personal protection gear. I stopped them: "You keep your gear on," I said. "I'll stand behind you." Why not, I figured—they were the guys with the guns.

I told them I had to get the rest of my guys into their gear and safety between trucks in the staging area. The troops said they'd do that after they took care of some other business. That wasn't the answer I wanted. "These guys are my responsibility," I said. "You can either take me to them now, or let me out and I'll walk."

The troops brought me to the staging area. The troops said they'd come back as soon as they found out what was going on, but pretty soon we got word that everything was okay. Somebody had spotted an unauthorized vehicle near the mess hall, and that's why the order to evacuate had been issued.

Figuring that was enough excitement for one night, I headed for the showers, with Richard acting as my personal escort. I never walked alone in camp at night. Some guy told us that we were supposed to be in our bunkers because the camp was under a bomb threat. I told him my guys were taken care of, and that I was going to take a shower.

As I was washing my hair, I heard Richard's voice from my radio just outside the shower. "Cindy, are you there?" I stepped outside the shower stall, grabbed the radio, and asked him if there was a problem. "The camp manager says we have to get to a bunker ASAP," Richard said.

CYNTHIA I. MORGAN

I rinsed off as best I could and started getting dressed quickly. I heard Richard's voice again.

"Cindy, are you there?"

What now?

"You can finish your shower," he said. Everything was fine. False alarm.

I won't repeat what I told him.

My second assignment as a solo CC came a couple of days later, after we returned to Anaconda. This convoy was headed back south to Kuwait. Once again, we were lucky to have great escorts, military police from the Sixteenth Airborne. When we got stuck in traffic on a highway near Baghdad code-named Sword, the MPs moved out and got the civilian cars out of the way. They also brought up two big dump trucks loaded with rocks and positioned them near to me, so I'd be better protected while we were stopped. This pissed me off for a couple of reasons. First, the trucks had been sitting beside two of my guys, which protected them—and now they moved the trucks to protect me. Why? And to make this even more ridiculous, the rock trucks blocked my view of the nearby rooftops. I had been watching them very carefully, looking for troublemakers.

I stuck my head out the window and yelled to a sergeant. "Hey, Sarge, why did you move those trucks. I can't see now."

The sergeant had been an escort for me before, and

he knew how I felt about being treated differently because of my sex. He walked over with a knowing look on his face. "Now you're protected," he said.

"Yeah, but those trucks were protecting *two* of my guys."

"Yes, ma'am," the sergeant replied. "But you can't argue with me on this one."

"Why not?"

"Because the American public can handle those other guys getting shot a lot better than if you get shot."

Well, this was a load of bullshit and I told him that, but nothing I said was going to change his mind.

We were stopped dead for an hour until the MPs cleared the road. Sword was one of the deadliest roads in Iraq, and there we were, immobile—just sitting there, with nowhere to go.

We had a tanker convoy in front of us, with civilian traffic between us. The tankers were especially vulnerable to attacks. We shouldn't have been surprised to find out that our escorts found an IED by the roadside about a hundred yards from where we were stopped. That IED may have been meant for us.

The military got the civilians out of the way, and we got rolling. As we approached the area where they found the IED, we veered to the left as far as we could—the bomb was on the right of the roadside. Our escorts were nervous because a day earlier they were with a convoy when an IED went off, severely wounding a civilian driver. I think that's part of the reason they moved those rock trucks to protect me when we were stopped.

The bloodshed continued in early April. Westerners were being kidnapped all over the country. Eighteen of our troops were killed in a single day, April 6. Two days later, a convoy was attacked and a driver was killed. The following day, one of our fuel convoys was ambushed west of Baghdad. Seven of my colleagues at KBR were taken hostage along with a soldier. One of the KBR drivers, Tommy Hamill, was paraded in front of television cameras on Al Jazeera and threatened with murder if the U.S. didn't immediately pull back from the offensive in Fallujah.

The other drivers were not identified—that was Halliburton's policy—so I was worried that friends of mine might have been part of that convoy. I hadn't heard anything from two friends in particular, so I emailed the company and asked if they were part of the ambushed convoy. Halliburton said they weren't, but I was still worried about them. KBR wouldn't tell us anything—they just said that the roads were shut and that a couple of convoys had been hit. Meanwhile there were plenty of rumors making the rounds. Finally the company called us together and told us what had happened to that convoy, but nobody mentioned names. What's stunning is that I was getting better information from my family back home than I was from KBR in Iraq. When we tuned to CNN in camp, reports from Iraq were broadcast without any sound—that wasn't KBR's policy, but somebody somewhere was censoring the news. I'd call my father back in the States, and we'd be watching the same broadcast at the same time, except he could hear the reports, and I couldn't. It was unbelievably frustrating.

The fighting continued in and around Fallujah, but the terrorists didn't kill Tommy Hamill. They killed everybody else, though. A couple of weeks later, the bodies of the four KBR drivers and of Sgt. Elmer Krause were found in shallow graves near the site of the ambush. The whereabouts of the two other KBR drivers, along with Hamill, were unknown.

Before the war, Hamill was a dairy farmer in Mississippi who was deep in debt. He joined KBR because he wanted to pay off his debts and maybe have a little money in the bank for a change. Like any of us, he never thought he'd wind up being dragged off into captivity by terrorists who wouldn't think twice about slitting his throat in front of a camera.

We didn't hear any more about Tommy after he became the most famous contractor in Iraq. But in early May, he was back in the news, and the news was good. Tommy had escaped from his captors and flagged down a U.S. military convoy. It actually was the second time he had gotten himself free, but the first time he couldn't find any U.S. troops before he was recaptured. It's amazing that they didn't kill him on the spot.

With the massacre of the four Blackwater contractors in late March and now the loss of six KBR contractors, Americans were becoming aware of the vital role civilians were playing in supplying our men and women in uniform. People were learning for the first time, a year into the war, the undeniable fact that our military couldn't do the job alone. It was up to contractors like KBR to provide the equipment and personnel to keep the troops supplied and fed.

One news account noted that we ate in the mess halls, shopped at the PX, and slept in camps, but we were not considered combatants. So the question was whether we were fair game for the terrorists. By April, nearly sixty Halliburton employees had been killed in Iraq or Kuwait, and another hundred had been wounded. A lot of commentators in the States were saying that we were mercenaries trying to make money off the war. If we were killed or hurt, well, we shouldn't be considered innocent civilians. It didn't seem to occur to some observers that all

Americans were fair game to the terrorists, whether we were in uniform in Fallujah, driving a truck outside Baghdad, or working as a waiter in the restaurant at the top of the World Trade Center.

In the midst of the carnage, news broke about the abuse of prisoners in Abu Ghraib prison in Baghdad. Again, we didn't get many of the details—only what we heard on the Armed Forces Radio Network—but we knew enough to be angry and appalled. By the same token, so many of us were getting shot at that we didn't have the time or energy to focus on the scandal. We were just trying to make it from convoy to convoy. We knew that the prison abuse story was going to make our jobs a lot more dangerous. There would be some kind of payback. The terrorists would do something awful and call it revenge for Abu Ghraib.

My Yahoo discussion group was generating a lot of attention on the web. People other than just my friends and family were registering and offering lots of positive comments. They were getting a glimpse of life inside a family that had a loved one in the war zone. I also thought the group might help people understand that not all civilian contractors are money-hungry mercenaries, like so many of the war's critics were saying, and there was a lot of good going on in Iraq.

I found that I was building an audience for my blog, and that people were eager to hear another side of the story in Iraq. The irony was that people in the States were hearing about the bad news—the attacks on convoys, for example—and we weren't. And we were hearing and witnessing the good things, but the folks back home weren't learning about that side of the war.

In the midst of all this, my oldest boy, nineteen-year-old Kenny, found out that he might be deployed to Iraq in the fall. He posted an email on my website, letting people know that he might be joining me. He added that his unit in the Arkansas National Guard was already in Iraq, attached to the Thirty-ninth Infantry Brigade, but he hadn't been able to join them because he hadn't finished his infantry training yet.

I sent Kenny an email telling him that I was proud of him, and that regardless of what new unit he was assigned to, he'd very quickly think of his fellow soldiers as family. That's what happened to me, I wrote.

> I know that you and your unit are a
> family and you would like to stay with
> them, but I have found that there are sev-

eral families to be found over here. Several
of the escorts I have had have become my
friends. I know that you will do well with
the next unit you are with. It won't take
long for you to become part of their
family . . . When you have a close group
of people, in a situation like over here, you
never forget them.

Kenny understood what I meant. But the subject of family hit close to home. After all, Kenny already had family in Iraq. And he clearly had been thinking about that, and playing out how that might work out. He sent me this email:

To be truthful, I am a little scared
about being deployed, but I know that I
can trust my fellow soldiers. I want you
to also know that there won't be a great
chance for us to see each other because
you are my mom and I am your son, and
if we do meet or I am a part of your escort—I hate to say this and I know this is
going to sound heartless—but if I am a
part of your escort, I will not look at you
as my mom until the mission is over . . .
The reason for this is so that it won't in-

terfere with my mission. I love you, but I
hope you understand. I know this isn't
good to think about this, but I want you
to do this in case I do get deployed and I
do end up a part of your escort. If something happens to me, I want you to
grieve and mourn AFTER the mission is
complete, because I will do the same. I
know it will be tough, but it is for the
well being of the soldiers and the
civilians.

I was in my villa in Kuwait when I got that email. I
was in tears as I read it. While I could understand
Kenny's point, I wasn't sure that I could be a CC first and
a mom second. But that was what he was asking me to
do. So many times I had looked at the young soldiers
serving in Iraq and said to myself, "That could be my
son." I thought I could handle his deployment to Iraq
when it was just a possibility, but now that it seemed
likely, I wasn't so sure anymore. I was scared for him and
for myself. His email really tore me up. Part of why I went
to Iraq was to do for someone else's son or daughter what
I hoped someone would do for my son one day. Now it
looked like I might actually be doing it for my son. That
was weird, scary, and difficult to think about.

I responded:

If you are deployed after your training, I hope that the only times we meet are in camps and never outside the wire. And for the reasons you state in your email, if you are ever to be one of my escorts, I will request that you or I be removed from the convoy. I know that you will understand my reasoning for that. Whereas they may be able to train you to not look at me as your mom but as another American, I am not sure that I could do the same. Every person I take with me on a mission is very important to me. If I make the wrong decision, it could get them or myself killed. Every man and woman that chooses to cross the wire on a mission with me is my responsibility. They are MY guys and gals . . . So if something were to happen and you were on my escort team, I am not sure that I could not think of you first and them later. They need to be first in my mind. Besides, this family does not need to lose two people at one time over here. Things are getting hotter over here day by day. Today they shut down all movement in Iraq . . . I am in Kuwait right now and waiting for word on several friends that are still in Iraq. I am going nuts! I have three friends that are CCs and should have been in the Baghdad area today . . . I can see your uncomfortable feelings about coming over here and totally understand them. I get them myself sometimes. But I know in my heart that we, as a nation, are doing the right thing by being here. You are my hero, as are all the other soldiers. I am so very proud of you. So if you find yourself over here, doing escorts, and one day you walk out to find me sitting in the lead truck of the convoy you are to escort, please understand that I love you and it will not be a lack of feeling secure with you that makes me request another escort team, but the concern of a mother for her son.

In Kenny's reply, he said that if he found out that I was in a convoy he had to protect, he "will not, and I repeat, WILL NOT, let you know that I am a part of your escort."

He was one tough soldier. He was going to treat me like he would anybody else. And in a weird way, that's all I wanted from the troops and from my fellow workers—to be treated just like anybody else.

Of course, the troops and my drivers weren't my sons.

FIVE

ALMOST NOTHING WAS MOVING
in Iraq in late April. The fighting,
especially in the north, was so intense that we were kept
off the roads. Back in the States, everybody was talking
about the prison abuse scandal as shocking photos of

some of the abuse were being published in the media. But we were paying closer attention to the offensive against the followers of the radical cleric Muqtada al-Sadr, who was leading a revolt in Najaf. Meanwhile, British troops in Basra were coming under attack from Sadr's loyalists in the south.

Many people back home, seeing only the negative, were beginning to wonder about our mission in Iraq. And people like the Syrian president, who was looking the other way while terrorists slipped into Iraq from his country, were saying that we had failed to liberate Iraq. Tell that to people who lived in fear under Saddam.

I was back in my villa in Kuwait, waiting for a new assignment, sending emails home and staying in touch with Ed via email. I had fallen for him big time, despite myself. After Jack, I wasn't looking to get involved with somebody again. But Ed had been so kind to me, and after I was attacked, he got me through the emotional pain and terror. Unlike most of the men I had known in my life, he seemed genuinely interested in me as a person.

We finally got rolling again in early May, but the situation in Iraq was still very tense. But there was good news, too. On May 2, Tommy Hamill managed to escape from his captors and was rescued by U.S. soldiers. We all let out hoots and hollers when we heard about his escape over the radio. A lot of us figured he was dead. We had heard rumors that his headless body had been strapped to

The last picture taken of me and my boys—Steffan, Kenny, and Ian—before I left for Iraq.

Trying on my flak vest and helmet shortly after arriving.

The photo on the right was my
Papaw's favorite;
he showed it to the nurses
in the hospital
right before he died.

The first time I ate out at the local market in Kuwait.

My windshield, the first time I was rocked.

Our convoys attracted the attention of Iraqi children. One little boy, Adgnon (left), stole my heart. He and his brother, Ida (right), shared the Peterbilt cap I gave him.

Papaw said he didn't know who was screaming more, me or the camel.

In full gear with my KBR truck.

In one of
Saddam's
carriages.

The guys gave me a hard time about my Christmas tree, but I told them, "It doesn't matter where you are on Christmas, we should all be celebrating. We are alive!" That said, it was the first Christmas I spent completely alone, without my family.

My favorite part was getting to know the soldiers I was there to help.

With some of the other "reefer" (refrigerator-truck) drivers.

In early February 2004, I was assigned the job of lead person, organizing the convoys and getting them moving. After I was attacked, I had to get back on the road. I had them pull the cage off my truck before I went on a mission—if you were in a rollover, you'd be trapped.

Me and part of my crew in the ancient city of Ur, playing tourist.

Our military escorts from the Twenty-first Airborne Military Police on a mission in March. One of our KBR personnel was severely wounded in an attack that day, but these guys got me and my crew through safely.

Our escorts from the 660th Transportation Company were delayed on our mission to and from Al Asad, but it was worth the wait. They were real pros.

Stopped in traffic on a highway code-named Sword, outside of Baghdad, one of the deadliest roads in Iraq. Our escorts found an IED (improvised explosive device) about a hundred yards from where we were stopped, in front of the building on the far right.

I spent the day I reported the attack to KBR security with Ed so I wouldn't have to go back to my room, where it had happened. That same day, I met Ollie North, who was passing through for one of his stories. *(Photo by Matt Lawson)*

With my crew at Scania, a camp about an hour and a half south of Baghdad.

Almost nothing was moving in late April 2004 because the fighting was so intense. This striker unit ran with us after they reopened the roads.

We handed out extra ice to the troops at a camp near Taji. They loved us for it.

With my crew and some of our shooters in early June 2004 at a camp code-named TQ/Ridgeway, near Fallujah, which had been the center of an insurgent rebellion earlier that spring.

Hanging out on the beach with some Marines at TQ on the sixtieth anniversary of D-Day. When you're in the desert, you don't always think to pack your trunks, so I just waded in.

With my crew at Camp Anaconda, about an hour north of Baghdad.

My friend Keith Nash, who told me about the job at KBR. He was also one of the first people I confided in about my attack in March.

The soldiers wanted a picture of me in the turret of this Humvee. As one of the few women drivers around, I got this kind of request a lot.

This is the crew I had when Roy Hawkins was shot during an ambush on the road from Anaconda to Kuwait. John Peay *(far left)*, is holding the bullet I dug out of the door after it went through Roy's leg. Robert Rowe *(far right)* took a bullet to the leg a few weeks later during a mission from Kuwait to Anaconda. *(Photo by Matt Lawson)*

I was delighted when I heard that Roy had fully recovered from his wound. *(Photo courtesy of Roy Hawkins)*

One of our trucks after a rear-end accident just south of Camp Cedar. The driver was knocked out of the truck, seat and all. I was just a passenger in this convoy, catching a ride back to Anaconda after spending three weeks in Kuwait talking to officials about my attack.
(Photos by Robert Easley)

On August 21, an ambush left this hole in my windshield, my driver Robert with a bullet in his left knee, and me with shrapnel in my right arm. Since I insisted on driving myself, Robert was in the passenger seat. The bullet had been meant for me. *(Photo by Tiger Six)*

the hood of a car and driven around by the terrorists. Tommy's plight had gotten a lot of attention because of his appearance on television.

My first mission in two weeks was a convoy to Anaconda. It was a trip I'd describe as routine and uneventful, but those words didn't mean the same anymore. What I considered routine before I came to Iraq bore no resemblance to what I now considered routine. The idea of having a shooter in my truck would have been crazy before I left the States. But now, I didn't give it a second thought, just as I didn't think anything of getting rocked, or hearing mortar shells explode.

That's not to say that nothing bothered me. I still got pissed off when I saw things that were just plain wrong, especially if they involved my guys. During a postmidnight bus ride to Arifjan, where we would pick up our trucks, I noticed that several of my guys looked tired. Of course, it was two o'clock in the morning, but even still, they really seemed exhausted, and I told them so. They conceded that they were as tired as they looked, because there were twelve to fifteen guys sleeping in a villa designed to accommodate about eight people. It was hard to get a decent night's sleep on a cot with that many people in the room.

I thought this was outrageous, and after we got our trucks and made the ninety-minute drive from Arifjan to Navistar, I called my boss and complained. There was no reason these guys should have been cramped like that. Lucky for us, these poor guys got a chance to take a nap at Navistar before we pushed on for Cedar, which was a ride of about two and a half hours.

We picked up our escorts at Cedar and headed out to Scania, where we had to drop off some ice. After we pulled in, I ran into one of the troops who had escorted us to Al Asad, and he spread the word that I was in camp. Before long, a bunch of them paid me a visit and told me that they had been thinking about me when they heard about the convoys getting hit. They also told me that their commanding officer had told them publicly that I had commended them for the job they did on the trip to Al Asad. They thanked me, and I thanked them. We're all on the same team.

For the next stage of this "routine" trip, we had a contingent of Marines with us. Before we left, we learned that insurgents had taken out a bridge we were supposed to cross for the trip toward Anaconda. We had to improvise another route.

Our convoy was one of four. The other three were tanker convoys, with fifteen trucks apiece, and they were a huge target. Our little seven-truck reefer convoy was in the middle, five minutes behind the lead convoy, and five minutes ahead of the convoy behind us. I put shooters in all of my trucks, including my own. Usually I didn't take a shooter in my truck because I rode right behind the lead gun truck. I figured that was enough protection for me. On this ride, however, the military insisted that I take a shooter as well. We were running a route we hadn't been on before, and it was dangerous.

Along the way, as we drove near a small town, I could hear the crackle of small-arms fire. My shooter was more nervous than I was. The gunfire, it turned out, wasn't from hostile forces. This was a Thursday evening, a time when weddings are celebrated all over Iraq. The gunfire was part of the ritual.

More ominous was a warning from our escorts that they had found an IED along the roadside. We were told to cross over a divided highway to get around the bomb. Not long afterward, we had to cross a pontoon bridge, which was a challenge for some of my guys—four of them messed up their bumpers trying to ease their way onto the structure. It was a long ride, and we finally pulled into Anaconda long after sunset.

In Iraq in the spring of 2004, this qualified as uneventful.

The tension was beginning to gnaw at people. While my truck was undergoing routine inspection at Anaconda, I chatted with some tanker drivers who said they were short-handed and needed five drivers to run a mission. I heard that about three hundred drivers, maybe as many as five hundred, had packed up and gone home since the fighting escalated. The tankers were hard hit, because the terrorists were especially targeting them. One guy refused to be reassigned to tanker duty and was fired.

Later on that day, the tankers were looking for a driver for a mission to Camp Ridgeway in Fallujah. One of my guys refused the assignment, and the foreman threatened to send him to the company's human resources department—which would have led to his getting fired. I told the foreman, a guy named Charles, that before he got any of my guys fired, I'd go in his place. I told him I was not about to lose good drivers over a stupid disagreement. Some of these guys had small kids at home, and most of them would have pulled anything to Ridgeway except a tanker.

The foreman and supervisor got everybody together and said he still needed a volunteer to drive a tanker to Fallujah. I asked a few pointed questions: Could they guarantee that this would be a one-time-only mission? If they didn't get a volunteer, would they assign somebody to do it? And if that person refused, would he be reported to Human Resources?

The answer to all three questions was the same: Yes.

Charles, the foreman, looked at me. I knew he was thinking about our previous conversation. I returned his look and said, "You know what we talked about." I didn't want to make a scene in front of my guys—I didn't want them to know that I had said I would take the tanker job if nobody else volunteered.

Charles nodded and asked me to go to the office with him. When I told him earlier that I would take the tanker job if nobody else would, Charles said he wasn't sure he could give it to a CC. I told him he'd have to make it happen if it came to that. As we got to his office, he opened the door and told the guys inside that he had a volunteer for the tanker job, and that "she's a CC."

I don't know if it was because I was a woman, or because I was a CC, or maybe they were simply telling the truth, but the other guys in the office immediately said they already had found a volunteer on their own, and that my services would not be required.

I went back to my guys, who were wondering what the hell was going on. I told them there was nothing to worry about, that everything was settled. They knew there was more to the story, so they kept asking me questions until I finally told them what had been going on behind the scenes. The guy who refused the mission pulled me aside and said he'd have never forgiven himself if I went in his place and got hurt or killed.

"It was my decision to go, not yours." I told them. "You have no reason to feel bad about it."

They said the foreman would have had hell to pay if something had happened to me. I didn't want to hear that. "Look, he's just doing his job," I said. Charles was a good guy. I met him in Houston way back when we were training for this job, and I knew he didn't want to send me on the tanker convoy. But that didn't matter.

We were stuck in Anaconda for a while, and I was going stir-crazy—but my boredom was magnified by disability. I had hurt my left knee when I slipped while hooking up my air lines, which are part of the truck's braking system It's part of the routine drivers follow when they're hooking up a trailer to move it. I lost my balance and fell on the corner of the truck frame. I had to be helped off the catwalk I was standing on because my leg was numb—I had landed squarely on my kneecap. I wound up with a cut and a pretty bad bruise on my kneecap, bad enough that I couldn't drive for a couple of days. I still could serve as a CC, but I had to have a driver with me—actually, KBR wanted all CCs to have drivers now, but reefer CCs were the last holdouts. We hated the idea of having a driver. We were driving some of the most dangerous roads in the world. If a driver messed up and ran over a bomb, you were dead. If bullets started flying, a driver had to stay calm and listen to the CC's orders; otherwise everybody would be at risk. Would you want somebody else driving you under those conditions? We wanted to drive ourselves.

After a couple of days, I brought some ice to a small camp six kilometers outside Anaconda. Because of my knee, I had a driver with me, a guy named Ted. We had a blast, in part because the troops were so grateful. They hadn't ever gotten any edible ice before, and we made sure they had more than enough to last them for a while. Even so, we had four pallets of ice left over after we filled their ground unit, and I wasn't about to take any ice back with me if it could be avoided. Word got around that we had ice, and more and more soldiers asked us for some. There were about a thousand troops in this camp, and we told them we'd make the rounds and hand out ice to anybody who wanted some. Ted and I spent the day hitting all the bunkers, tents, and medical units. One soldier told me that they had just gotten their freezer hooked up. Would I mind if they filled it up with ice? I told them to take all the ice they wanted.

It was fantastic—the kind of day that made my job worth it. It's hard to grasp this, but a simple thing like ice put smiles on the faces of these soldiers. Put yourself in their places: You're in a forward operating base in a desert, it's a hundred and five degrees, but you can't consume any of the little ice you have because it's made from local water—and that water isn't fit for consumption.

Then along come Ted and me, and we've got all the ice you need and then some.

A couple of days later, we set out for a much larger camp near Taji, where about twelve thousand troops were based. Normally the drive from Anaconda to Taji should take about twenty minutes. It took us hours. The road from Anaconda to Taji, code-named MSR (Military Supply Route) Tampa, was notorious for roadside explosives. Convoys were getting hit along that road every day. We were delayed because our escorts found an IED, and we had to wait until we got the all-clear.

At Taji, some troops had gone four days without even a small bag of ice. We loaded it into the storage trailer, although we handed out some extras to the troops who came by and asked.

These were really worthwhile days, but the work of unloading was beginning to show. Getting up and down from the truck put a strain on my bad knee, and I felt it. I had to see a medic when I got back to my villa in Kuwait. I was told to take it easy for a while. For me, that was more easily said than done.

I was sinking into a pit of depression. My medical condition was getting me down. While my knee was getting better, it wasn't getting better fast enough. On May 14, the medic said I could go back to work, but only on light duty. That meant no bending, no kneeling, and no use of my lower left leg. That pretty much meant that I couldn't do anything except sit on my tail. And if that didn't help after three days, they told me I'd have to get the knee X-rayed.

I was scared that there was something wrong with the knee beyond just a bruise. And I was scared that the doctors would send me home—I had heard stories of drivers who got hurt and were sent home for good. But I loved what I was doing in Iraq. I felt I had found my calling. I didn't want this new life I had made for myself to end, all because of a stupid injury.

I wrote another email to Ed: "I wish you would get here to help me with this." Ed assured me that he was doing everything in his power to get free and come to see me. He was on a mission in northern Iraq, and reefer convoys were having trouble getting escorts because their convoys were only seven trucks, instead of the usual fifteen or more. The military didn't want to "waste" escorts on a small convoy, so Ed had to wait for other trucks to fill out the slots.

On the evening of May 16, 2004, I was at the medic's office, getting my knee checked out. It was still pretty sore. The medic and I got to talking about the recent murder of Nick Berg, a twenty-six-year-old contractor from Pennsylvania who had been taken hostage in April and then was beheaded by the terrorists in Iraq. The medic mentioned that he had seen the ghastly video of the murder and had a copy of it on his computer. He asked me and a couple of other people in the office if we wanted to see it. I did, but I didn't. I knew what had happened to poor Nick Berg, and knew that the terrorists had recorded their atrocity and posted it on websites. But I hadn't seen it. I decided that maybe I ought to see it, just to remind me of the kind of enemy we were fighting in Iraq. I knew it would be awful, and I knew I'd be sick after seeing this poor guy's life taken away from him in a terrible way.

We gathered around the medic's computer. I'll never forget what I saw and heard, and I hope that I never see or hear anything like it again.

The video was sickening. Nick, dressed in an orange jumpsuit, was sitting on the floor, with a pack of hooded monsters behind him. He was forced to read a statement, and then one of the monsters produced a huge knife, grabbed him by the hair, cut off his head, and held it up. As grisly as this sight was, the sounds were even worse. I can still hear them now—the sound of Nick screaming, and when that stopped, the sound of the blood gurgling in his throat as they sawed off his head. It was not just an execution. It was torture.

I wasn't prepared for this. After it was over, we just walked away from the computer, speechless with anger and grief. The medic said every American ought to see this video. He thought that seeing this video would make Americans forget about the prisoner-abuse story.

I didn't agree with my friend. I didn't think anybody should see these terrible images. That night, I went back home and sent a long email to my friends and family, and posted it on my Yahoo discussion group. I mentioned that I had said from the outset that my discussion group was a place for me to talk about my experiences, and not to debate the politics of our presence in Iraq. But I had to break that rule for this occasion.

I wrote:

> Seeing this video is part of my experience and as much as it makes me want to ask myself what in the hell I am doing here, and if I should really share this with you, I told ya'll that I would not hide anything from you and would give ya'll the truth.
>
> Please, please, if any of you have not seen this video, DON'T! It is a gruesome

thing to watch and I cannot see how any human being can do something like that to another. I sit here and have tears running down my face. I feel for his family and those that knew him. I am deeply saddened that there are such monsters in this world. And that is what they are, monsters!

I came here thinking that we were doing the right thing, that we were helping these people. I still believe that. I don't think that will change. I just wish that the American people would stop all their whining and bitching about this and that and let the military do what needs to be done here . . . No one deserved to die that way, no one. You think that 9/11 was bad because of the body count. This one death, to me, was just as bad if not worse.

I will never get the image of what I saw out of my head, and neither will any of us that were here tonight. I want to see our government doing something about this. I want retribution for my fellow Americans that had to die in such a manner that it will give us nightmare images for the rest of our lives.

Yes, war is costly, in more ways than one. It costs money, and it costs the lives of our brothers, sisters, parents, and children. It cost some of us more than that. It costs some of us our own lives. We know when we step on that plane to come over here that we could be killed by any number of things, but not that way. Not like that.

As I typed this message, I was still crying. I didn't know what to feel, and at the same time, I felt a powerful mixture of emotions—anger, sadness, and fear, a feeling of being thankful and of being more determined.

I tried to explain all of this in my email:

Anger: I am so very angry that this happened to a fellow human being. It doesn't matter where he came from, what color his skin is, what religion he practices. He was a human being and deserved better than that.

Sadness: For the family and friends that knew this man. I can't say that I understand their pain, and I hope that is something I will never be able to understand.

Fear: I never will allow myself to be taken hostage. I know this may disturb ya'll, but I won't go through what they did to the people they have taken hostage.

Thankfulness: Now this is one that I have a hard time dealing with. I am thankful it wasn't me or one of my friends. I know that I should not be ashamed to feel this feeling, but it some ways, it feels wrong to be thinking that.

More determined: Hell, yes, I am more determined to stay here and do my part to support our troops to rid the world of monsters like that. They are not human. They cannot be allowed to go on doing this.

They have to be stopped.

I knew this email would disturb many people at home, but I also felt these things had to be said. And I meant every word of it, particularly the bit about not being taken hostage.

I had seen enough to know I would not let myself be taken hostage. If I came under attack, they'd have to kill me. I had only one weapon—my truck. I'd run over as many of them as I could, and if for some reason I was forced to abandon my truck, I'd fight and cause so much trouble that they'd put a bullet in my head rather than bother taking me hostage.

All of us who saw that video agreed to send emails home, or call our families, and ask them to stay away from the Berg video. We agreed it would cause our loved ones far too much anguish. I was too late with the email for two of my boys. Kenny sent me an email, telling me that he and Steffan had seen the video. I immediately called them to see how they were handling it, especially knowing that their mom was in the war zone. Both boys were angry beyond words. Kenny wanted to get over there even more than before. But neither one of them asked me to come home. In a way, I was surprised, but then again, I wasn't. They knew, as much as I did, that I had found a purpose in my life, that I was dedicated to helping the troops who were protecting our freedom.

I did tell Kenny that I would never let the terrorists take me alive. I told them what I had told myself: that they'd have to kill me, then and there. He didn't want to hear that. "If you die," he said, "I'll be on the first plane over there and I'll go hunting for them. Nobody will stop me."

That scared me. I didn't want my son flying to Iraq to avenge my death. Still I wouldn't let that fear gnaw at me. I had to stay, even though it was dangerous. I really believed that I was not destined to die in Iraq.

I was more determined than ever to stay in Iraq and get the job done.

There was, however, a slight problem: My knee was acting up, and I was about to be sent home.

A doctor at the International Clinic in Kuwait wanted me to get an MRI back in the States. There still was fluid on the knee, and I developed a burning sensation whenever I used the leg for a bit. The knee also felt like it was out of place half the time.

I sent an email home the day after I saw the Berg video, letting folks know that I would be on my way to my father's house in Tennessee in a matter of days. That no doubt came as a relief to my friends and family, especially after my email of the previous night.

I left Kuwait on May 18 for what turned out to be a tough flight to Tennessee via Amsterdam and Detroit. The knee was very cranky from all that sitting. One of the first things I did when I got to my father's house was unpack a tapestry that Ed had bought for me in Kuwait and lay it out on my bed. The tapestry, in varying shades of blue and slate, was a constant reminder of Ed and how much he meant to me. Ed had sent an email that disturbed me. Ed said that his convoy was going well but he had a bad feeling—something bad was in the air, he said. "I just can't put my finger on it," he said. "Something just isn't right."

Reading about Ed's premonition left me feeling helpless and anxious. I thought of Ed as a tested and respected veteran. He wasn't somebody who panicked at the first sound of a mortar, or who paid much attention to rumors. If he felt that something wasn't right, I thought, it probably wasn't right. I chose not to pay attention to comments I had heard from other drivers, who said that Ed wasn't the veteran driver he said he was, and that I actually was a braver CC than he. Some of these same people also told me that Ed wasn't separated from his wife. I didn't listen to that either.

Things weren't going right with my knee. At first, the news seemed to be good: After an examination and an X-ray a doctor said he thought all I had was a bad contusion, although he ordered an MRI just to be safe. The news seemed good. I figured that if I stayed off the knee and really let it heal, I could be headed back to Kuwait in ten days or so. That made me very happy—I wanted to get back there as quickly as I could. But that's when I ran into a wall of red tape. I went for my MRI on a Friday morning, and then found out that my doctor was going to be out of the office the following week. If he saw anything he didn't like in the MRI, he wouldn't be able to treat it for a week and a half. I was stunned. "Look," I said, "I have to get back to Kuwait ASAP." I had visions of being stuck in the States for weeks, waiting for doctors and test results and being bored out of my mind.

Luckily, though, the doctor got the results before he left, and he let me know that his original diagnosis was correct. All I had was a bad contusion, and that meant that after a little rest, I'd be on my way back to where I belonged. That perked up my spirits considerably. In the meantime, though, I had to take it easy.

Out of nowhere one morning, I got a phone call from Bill. He was the last person I expected to hear from while I was home. One of my friends must have slipped him word that I was home.

He told me he needed to hear my voice. I suppose I should have hung up the phone, but I didn't. But I noticed that I didn't get that lump in my stomach I usually got when I talked to him. That, I thought, was a good sign. I really was getting over him.

He talked about some girl he was messing with. If he thought that would upset me, he was wrong. He asked me about a letter I had sent him, in which I told him that he had been holding me back from what I needed to do for myself. Did I mean that, he asked.

"Yes," I said. "I meant it." He seemed surprised.

The conversation was a lot like my last visit with him.

I came away feeling sorry for him. He was heading down-hill, and fast, and there was nothing I could do about it—and I didn't feel bad about that. I didn't allow myself to get sucked into his world. I got off the phone and didn't feel messed up at all. I still had everything I had when I picked up the phone—I had me.

While I was doing my best to get some rest, I was check-ing out a civilian website and noticed that somebody had posted a map of either the Green Zone in Baghdad or BIAP—frankly, I don't remember which. I do remember how furious I was. Here was information the terrorists would love to have, and somebody was posting it on a website where anybody could see it. I sent an email, and to my surprise, they posted it. Here's what I wrote:

> I know that the news can be irrespon-
> sible and put out maps of the area that we
> are working in, but I really didn't think I
> could see a picture of one here. I thought
> the idea was to keep us as safe as possi-
> ble. I won't even mark the maps of Iraq

that I give my family as to exactly where the camps are. I point out the general area and that is it. I know that you may think I am overreacting on this, and that is fine. But I live and work there. And I am so sick and tired of the bitching and complaining that some people do about the safety of the contractors and then put a map on the site for anyone to look up on the Internet.

I don't care if it is in 1,000 other places, you don't have to do it here, and then complain that you are concerned over our safety. And as far as the safety of the guys AND gals over there driving trucks, if you don't feel it is safe enough, or are not willing to take the risk to protect not just our freedom, but that of others we share this planet with, then get out and go home. You are not the military, you have a choice as to whether you want to be there or not.

I was happy to say my piece. I knew some people would be upset, or would think I was overreacting. I was prepared for that. But one reply shook me badly. It came from somebody who obviously knew a little bit about me—he literally knew where I lived in Kuwait. And it was clear that he did not share my view of the work we were doing in Iraq. It made me wonder what the hell this guy was doing there. It also made me wish, for a moment, that I had kept my mouth shut.

The writer addressed me as "Miss Cindy in Iraq," and made mention of the fact that I lived in an air-conditioned villa in Kuwait (true, but I wasn't living in the kind of luxury the writer implied). He said he was a truck driver, too, but he didn't "live quite as high on the hog."

After making me sound like I was a member of the Saudi royal family, he said that he had read my complaints about the emphasis on negative news. He found this "very amusing & quite creative."

"You say a lot of negativity is posted here," he wrote. "Well, most of what goes on over there is negative. The Iraqis did like us, but the longer this drags out, the truth is, the less they like us. It's NOT just outside terrorists. These are homegrown, helped by outsiders."

Then this guy got personal again, saying that I wouldn't be in Iraq if I had found a better-paying job in the States. "I have seen you over in Kuwait," this guy wrote, "& am not the only one who has noticed that your knee bothers you [conveniently—except this guy spelled it "confidently"] & when certain people are around."

Nice. So this guy claims that I'm living in luxury in Kuwait, and that I'm faking an injury. And this from another American in the war zone!

I was upset, and I felt stupid for posting my original message.

Ed was having a problem of his own. He was in the middle of sending me an instant message from Camp Scania when the place got hit by mortars. Ed's premonitions were about camps in the north, where most of the attacks were taking place, but Scania is in the south, closer to the Kuwait border. One of the shells hit a tent, severely injuring three soldiers. A mutual friend of ours suffered a concussion. Luckily, Ed was okay.

I was dying to get over there. But before I did, I had my boys over for a visit. We didn't have time to do much, but it was wonderful to see them.

It was finally time to go back to the war. I had a flight out of Nashville on May 26, connecting in Detroit and Amsterdam before landing in Kuwait.

While I was waiting for my first flight in Nashville, I was talking with a friend on my cell phone about returning to Kuwait and the work I was doing there. A woman approached me and said she had overheard some of the conversation.

"I just wanted to thank you," this stranger said.

"For what?" I said. I really had no idea what she was talking about. Did she mistake me for somebody else? Did she overhear some other conversation and get mixed up?

"For doing what you're doing," she said. "We have some people over there and I'm glad to hear that there's somebody like you is there doing what you do. It's great to know that there are good people making sure that our guys are taken care of. God bless you."

With that, she gave me a great big hug. I could see she had tears in her eyes. Only then did she tell me that she had two grandsons serving in Iraq.

So I thanked her and wished her the best.

A few people overheard our conversation and approached me after the woman left for her flight. They asked me a lot of questions, and that gave me a chance to tell them what was really going on over there.

A few hours later, after I landed in Detroit, I was stopped by another woman who noticed I was wearing a shirt that had the words "Operation Iraqi Freedom" on the front. She was full of questions. She had this look of awe on her face that embarrassed me.

I wanted to tell her, look, I'm not a hero. I'm just one person doing a job that needs to be done.

Our soldiers are the heroes. And I was on my way back to give them a hand.

SIX

I WAS GLAD TO BE BACK IN IRAQ.
My buddies there felt like family by
now, and I was dying to see Ed.

I learned a long time ago about what happens when
you get diesel fumes in your blood. You're never really the

same again—you're a truck driver, and nothing else gives you the same satisfaction or freedom. Well, I guess being in Iraq added to that mixture of blood and diesel fumes. I don't know what you'd call it—the adrenaline rush of being in a war zone, or the pure excitement of being in a dangerous place. Whatever it was, it was preferable to sitting around at home, watching videos with my knee elevated.

The knee survived its first test—the long flight from Memphis to Kuwait, via Detroit and Amsterdam. I was a little concerned about how I'd feel during the two longest legs of the trip, but everything was fine. As we came in for a landing, I looked out the window. Those same colorful lights that I'd looked at in bewilderment the first time I flew in now said "Welcome home." True, Kuwait was not my real home. The way of life there was different, and it was dangerous. But still, as the plane landed, I couldn't help feeling that I was home.

Ed picked me up in Kuwait. It was wonderful to see him again, and even more wonderful that we would be together for my first mission since returning. I was his driver for a mission from Kuwait north to Anaconda, which had become the main center of operations for reefer drivers while I was in the States recuperating. It is astonishing to think that I was on a sofa in Tennessee in late May, and by early June I was back on the road in Iraq, surrounded not by friends and family but sand and more sand. I guess this is what people mean when they say we live in a global village. One minute you're watching a war movie in your den in the States, and the next minute you're driving through a war zone in the Middle East with a military escort, watching bombs fall and bullets fly for real.

It didn't take long for me to get back into the swing of things. Seeing the Iraqi kids waving to me along the roadside, watching camels and sheep watching us as we drove by, even checking out the spiderweb scars on truck windshields—all of this made me feel like I was back where I was supposed to be.

Once we got to Anaconda on June 3, I prepared myself for a confrontation with the reefer supervisors there. I had been told I'd have to sleep in a tent in Anaconda, but I decided that just wasn't going to happen. I wasn't going to sleep in a place where I couldn't lock a door—not after what had happened to me.

I took Ed with me for moral support and put in my request for a hooch—basically, a small room—instead of a tent. I explained why and was referred to a woman who said she understood my fear and pain, because she was a rape victim herself. But even still, she said, she had no hooch for me.

Ed asked me to leave so he could speak with her in private. When he emerged, he told me that I could have what they called a "dry hooch"—a room without a bathroom. I'd have to walk outside for a shower, but I could sleep behind a locked door. Ed never told me how he managed this one.

I was happy to have the hooch, but I found myself constantly volunteering for missions. I still felt the trauma of that violation, that assault on my body and my spirit. I felt protected in my truck.

I volunteered for a round-trip mission to a camp code-named TQ/Ridgeway near Fallujah. That city had been the center of an insurgent rebellion earlier in the spring. Ed was upset with me for volunteering for such a dangerous mission. I guess I could understand his point, but my view was this: I hadn't been to this camp in all my travels so far. And, since I considered myself a tourist who happened to drive a truck in a war zone, why not check out a new camp?

Getting there wasn't so easy. Reefer drivers were having a hard time getting escorts because we weren't considered a full convoy, and with hostilities flaring up, the military didn't feel it could spare an escort for anything less than a full convoy of fifteen or more trucks. I was pretty frustrated, and made my case to a general. I told him that the troops in Ridgeway were running out of ice, so we needed to deliver some as soon as possible. The general told me to speak to the brass in V Corps, which I did. It worked—my reefers were assigned to a flatbed convoy, which had to cut the number of its trucks to accommodate us.

Before we got on the road, I sat in on a KBR security briefing. There I was told that the road we were going to take, code-named Mobile, had just been designated Code Black, which meant that nobody was allowed on the road. So the main route from Anaconda to Fallujah was a no-go area. Another route, Sword, was Code Red—slightly safer than the main route, but not by a lot.

After the briefing, I met with the CC of the flatbed convoy we'd be riding with, a guy named Homer. We were briefed by the military, and they explained the route we were taking. Eventually, they said, we'd be on Sword, and then Mobile. I was a little confused about this—I asked Homer if he had heard what I heard about Sword and Mobile. He pretty much told me to stop worrying and just get in my truck.

We got ready to roll, although I still was confused and worried. I got on my radio and called Ed, who was elsewhere in camp. I told him to switch to a different channel, and when he did, I rattled off the route we were supposed to be taking and told him of my concerns. Not longer afterward, a voice on the radio said that the routes should not be mentioned in radio conversations. I had messed up—in my anxiety and confusion, I had identified the routes over the air. It was a breach of security.

I stopped talking. I was paralyzed with guilt. Ed realized what was going on and he quickly came to my truck and told me not to worry. "You have to keep your mind on the mission," he said. He was right, but I was in tears. What a stupid mistake! I just hate screwing up. When Ed left, I said a prayer for the mission. If anything went wrong, it would be my fault.

Thankfully there were no problems during the ride to TQ/Ridgeway. We got there safely and even got a chance to swim. Well, some of the guys did anyway, in a lake adjacent to the camp. I didn't have my gear—when you're in the desert, you don't always think to pack your swimming trunks!—so I just waded in the water. While I was in the truck on my way to the beach, I was listening to the news on Armed Forces Radio. President Bush was in France on this day, June 6, the sixtieth anniversary of D-Day. The announcer said that the president had been joined by President Jacques Chirac of France, who said that his country would never forget the sacrifice of American soldiers who gave their lives so that France could be free again. I hope that sixty years from now, Iraqis will be saying the same thing about the men and women who have given their lives in Operation Iraqi Freedom.

The following morning, the flatbed convoy, led by Homer, pulled out of camp without me and my guys. That meant I had to get my own military escorts for the trip back to Anaconda, via another camp where we had to drop off some ice. I found some Marines who were willing to do the job. In smaller camps, like Ridgeway, escorts weren't always readily available. All camps had what the military called a Movement Control Team to coordinate escorts with convoys, but often the MCTs took a while to find an escort unit. If you didn't feel like sitting around and waiting, you could ask to join a military convoy— whatever it took to get rolling, that's what you did. On this occasion, I was lucky enough to find the Marines to get us moving again.

We started on the first leg of our trip, from Ridgeway, which is south of the main city, to MEK/Camp Fallujah, which is north of the city, after dark on June 11. The two camps are only about eleven miles apart—that is, if you drive through the city. We weren't allowed to do that. We had to drive around the city. We figured it would take about three hours to get from one camp to the other.

We weren't thrilled about driving at night. But the military believed that if we kept running convoys 24/7 around Fallujah, the insurgents wouldn't get a chance to plant a long daisy chain of IEDs under the cover of darkness. If we were barreling through all night, they couldn't set up without being noticed. That seemed reasonable, but we drivers didn't like it. We couldn't see very well at night, and if we were running with any kind of lights on, we looked like a Christmas tree rolling down the road with a big sign that read, "Here I am, go ahead and shoot me."

We had no choice. We needed to get rolling, our escorts were Marines, and the Marines liked to run at night. As one officer told me: "The Army owns the day, but the Marines own the night."

After driving about ten kilometers, our escorts brought us to a halt, killed their lights, and told us to do the same. After a couple of minutes, we heard the thumping noise of helicopters overheard. *Oh, shit,* I was thinking. *What the hell did you get yourself and your guys into?* Remember, it was my decision to run with these Marines at night in a dangerous part of Iraq. And now we were stopped, and we could hear choppers, and that meant there was something in that darkness, something that was not friendly.

All of sudden they opened fire on an open field. They must have fired eight or even a dozen missiles at targets we couldn't see. I have to say I loved watching the fireworks. "This," I said, "is cool." They blew the hell out of whatever was in that field. And I'm happy to say we never found out what might have been waiting for us—the choppers took care of business, and we started rolling again. We pulled into Camp Fallujah around midnight.

The next day was god-awful hot. Horrible. Almost a hundred and twenty degrees. Days like this made me glad I worked in reefers (although, truthfully, I was always glad to be working in reefers). We spent an hour transferring ice into the trucks, but at least we were cool. After we were finished, I told one of my drivers to leave his unit running in the staging area and close one door. I then told our escorts, who were suffering in the intense heat and trying to sleep, that they could grab a nap in my driver's refrigerated unit. The sergeant said he had to stay with his Humvee, but that the rest of his troops could go to the truck. I told them they were all welcome. Word must have gotten out, because at one point that afternoon, when I stopped by to make sure it wasn't too cold, I found about thirty soldiers hanging out in the unit, sleeping, reading, or just taking a break from the heat.

Thanks to the kind of confusion and red tape that goes with being in a war, I was told I would have to make the drive from Anaconda to Ridgeway to pick up my trailer, which I had left at Ridgeway. It's enough to say that I was led to believe that I was supposed to drop the trailer there, but, well, somebody else thought differently.

I didn't particularly mind, because I liked what I saw at Ridgeway. I had hopes that I might even get a chance to go swimming this time.

I grabbed two other drivers to come with me to

Ridgeway and then tried to arrange for escorts. And then, because this is a war, we were forced to wait, and then wait some more. Not long after we finally got rolling, we got caught in a traffic jam in an area we called the "meat market." There were two good reasons for this nickname. First of all, it really was a meat market. It was a place where the locals butchered live animals on the side of the road. And then there was the other kind of slaughter, or at least the attempts to bring about slaughter. It was a no-toriously dangerous area for our convoys, and sure enough, I got rocked for the second day in a row—I also had been rocked on my way to Anaconda the day before. This time, whoever threw the rock had lousy aim. He hit the truck and not my windshield, which had gotten hit the previous day. By now, getting rocked was no big deal.

We got through the traffic jam and then headed to-ward Baghdad, driving on a new route I didn't know. When we were briefed before we left, the lieutenant in our escort unit said one of her guys had been on the route before. That was important. Official policy had it that at least one person in each escort unit had to have traveled the route before. Well, it turned out that Bagh-dad is a confusing city even for somebody who suppos-edly knew the route.

We got lost. Lost in Baghdad.

We made a series of U-turns, crossed a median, and I lost all sense of direction. It took a while before I recognized a mosque I had passed during an earlier trip to the city, so I knew that I had been in this area at least once before.

We kept making U-turns. Traffic was miserable—it was like a bad rush hour in any major American city, except that any of those cars next to you might be driven by a terrorist or a suicide bomber. I heard a guy on the radio say, "This is really starting to get on my nerves." Damn right. And I had to laugh, but not with any pleasure, when I heard somebody say that our escorts in front of us had stopped to get directions from some locals. Great.

I got on the radio and insisted that they take us to BIAP, where we could sort everything out. We knew we were making too much of a scene, driving aimlessly around this dangerous city and making too many U-turns.

Then, while we were on Sword—one of the most dangerous roads in Baghdad—I heard one of the flatbed drivers say he was taking fire on our left, and that he had been hit and the truck was losing power. This was happening somewhere in front of me, but I couldn't see or hear a thing.

I got on the radio and talked to my guys. "Ya'll keep following me," I told them. "Keep rollin'" They did. The two other reefer drivers and myself were in the back of the convoy, riding bobtail (because we were supposed to pick up our trailers in Ridgeway).

I saw the flatbed bobtail—the last flatbed driver in the line, right in front of me—pull over to his right to pick up the driver whose truck had been hit. While that rescue was under way, I led my guys around the damaged flatbed, which was on fire. I heard shots coming from our left, but nobody got hit.

The flatbed bobtail and the gun truck that was bringing up the rear eventually caught up with the rest of us, but there was more confusion to come. Our escorts missed the turn for BIAP, so we had to turn around again. By now, everybody was getting a little edgy. You could tell by the speeds they were hitting. The drivers ahead of us reefers were putting a little distance between themselves and me.

I could have caught up with the rest of the convoy, but I didn't want to leave my guys behind. I tried to maintain a speed where I could see the truck in front of me in the distance, and a truck behind me, driven by one of my guys. This wasn't so easy—at one point I had to run a red light so I wouldn't lose sight of the guys in front of me. I just plowed my way through the intersection and told my guys to do the same. Somehow we all made it though without hitting anyone, but it was close. I just missed a couple of small cars that crossed in front of me.

But I lost sight of the last flatbed just ahead of me. I got on the radio and told the CC of the flatbeds that I was separated from the convoy. "I'm gonna need some help,"

I said. "I don't know where ya'll are." I was nervous, because I was so turned around I didn't know where I was or what exit I was supposed to be looking for. But I made sure that when I talked to the flatbed CC, my voice didn't show any signs of anxiety.

The rest of the convoy slowed up and allowed us to catch up with them, which was a relief. We made one more U-turn, made the turn for BIAP, and pulled into the main gate.

I was pissed. We were led to believe that somebody on the convoy knew the way, but nobody did, and because of that, we could have gotten killed. We spent the day riding aimlessly around Baghdad—not exactly the place to be wandering around in June of 2004. This is how people wind up dead.

Once we were at BIAP, I called my supervisor and told him that I was going to pull my guys off the convoy and we'd find other escorts to take us to TQ/Ridgeway. I wasn't about to put the lives of my guys—guys who were my responsibility—on the line if this lieutenant wasn't going to do her job.

My supervisor told me to calm down, but he also was ready to back me up if I decided to pull my guys from the convoy.

We went to the staging area and I had a little talk with the lieutenant. It turned out that she didn't realize until we pulled into BIAP that we had left behind a truck engulfed in fire. Her part of the convoy had taken fire, too, and I think she was too busy reporting it instead of checking on the rest of the convoy.

I told the lieutenant straight out that if she didn't know the rest of the way to TQ/Ridgeway "for sure," I was going to pull my guys off the convoy and we'd find other escorts. She just looked at me and didn't say a word.

The CC for the flatbeds, a guy we called "Sweet Pea," spoke up and said he knew the way. He promised he could get us there. I called my supervisor back and told him that I still wasn't satisfied, and that I was going to find other escorts for my guys. He reassured me that Sweet Pea was a competent guy who really did know the way to Ridgeway. I grudgingly said I'd roll with the convoy as planned. But I didn't like it one bit.

I'm happy to note that Sweet Pea knew the way, and we got to TQ/Ridgeway without further incident—that is, except for three flat tires on the same military vehicle. Because of that, a ride that should have taken six hours at most took eleven hours. It was draining and exhausting, but at least nobody was shooting at us.

I learned a lot of things about human nature and war, and one of those things was that sometimes you just have to shake your head, because things happen that make no sense at all. And you wonder how some decisions get made, and you get pissed off because sometimes people pay the ultimate price because of a bad or stupid decision.

In late June, I grabbed two other guys for a run from Anaconda to MEK/Camp Fallujah by way of BIAP to deliver ice. We got to BIAP without any incidents, but we got stuck there for three days while we waited for a slot with a larger convoy. The only convoys moving between BIAP and Fallujah, a forty-five-minute drive, were carrying ammunition, and we weren't allowed to run in convoys hauling munitions. Finally, we were tucked into a military convoy heading toward Fallujah and talked some Marines into escorting us to the first checkpoint outside MEK/Camp Fallujah. We'd be on our own for the short drive between the first checkpoint and the camp gate.

My supervisor didn't care for the arrangement, but he agreed to it. I went back to my guys and explained the situation—anytime I wanted to do something that was out of the ordinary, or stretching the rules, I consulted my guys. They knew I had a tendency to push the envelope a little. But I wasn't about to say, "Look, I know this is unusual, but we're going to do it because I say so." I didn't run my convoys that way, although I had the authority to do so. "This is not a dictatorship," I told them before our missions. "Your opinions, thoughts, and ideas are welcomed." But I also reminded them: "I get to have the final say." The guys agreed with my plan to drive without escorts from the checkpoint to the camp gate.

So we left BIAP at night with the larger convoy, but as we passed Abu Ghraib prison, the lead escort and my three trucks pulled out of the line and got on the road leading to Camp Fallujah. When we got to the checkpoint, the escorts left us as planned. We continued on our way to the gate, which was just a few kilometers away. As we pulled up to the camp gate, the two soldiers on duty seemed surprised to see three Americans driving at night with no escorts. I explained to them that our escorts had brought us to the checkpoint and then left us—which is all I had asked them to do.

The soldiers clearly didn't approve. They said the escorts shouldn't have left us. I tried to explain that this was the deal I had cut with them. The two soldiers contacted a lieutenant and explained that they had three Americans at the gate without escorts. The lieutenant told the troops to tell us to go away.

Here we were, fellow Americans, drivers who put ourselves on the line to help the troops, and this lieutenant was telling us to go away. And where were we going to go?

I couldn't believe what I was being told. I told the

soldiers, "Look, we're Americans, and we're not going anywhere." One of the soldiers said he was sorry and explained that he couldn't let us inside the gate. But he also said he wasn't about to send us away, which is what the lieutenant wanted him to do. He directed us to a place outside the wire but right under a guard tower. We could park there overnight, he said, and we'd be protected by the guards.

It wasn't the best situation, but it was better than turning around and going—where? So we parked under the tower, outside the wire, and tried to get some sleep. About four hours later, all three of us were awakened by a knock on the cab door. "Get your stuff," I heard somebody say. "You're coming into camp." A bunch of troops in two Humvees had pulled up to take us inside the wire. The fact that they came out in their well-protected Humvees made me wonder how safe we actually were outside the camp.

It turned out that when guard duty changed shifts, the soldier who had told us where to park told the new shift's commanding officer what was going on—that three Americans were parked in trucks outside the camp. The CO told the troops to get us into camp, and the soldier who told us where to park was part of our little rescue party. He had felt bad that his lieutenant wouldn't let us into camp in the first place, and he wanted to make sure we were safe.

We were happy to be inside, but we also were tired. If we had any thought of getting back to a nice long sleep, however, we were mistaken. At about six o'clock in the morning, we were rudely awakened again, this time by mortar fire. A shell landed inside the camp, close enough that it shook me out of bed. I slipped on my shoes and stepped outside the tent. By now I knew the drill—when a shell hits nearby, you look for smoke to see how close it came, and to make sure nothing was hit. There was just a little smoke, so no harm done.

While I was checking it out, I ran into a sergeant I had met the last time I delivered ice to Camp Fallujah. He remembered me and asked me why I was sleeping in the tent. I told him what had happened when we arrived at the gate, and how we weren't allowed inside the wire. He was angry.

There was no getting back to sleep now, so the three of us asked to be taken back to our trucks. The sergeant who remembered me took us outside the gate. On the way, he asked me why I was in Iraq in the first place. I gave him the answer I had given other people, including myself. "I'm just a tourist," I said. "Driving a truck facilitates my tourism." He laughed.

"With an attitude like that," he said, "you should have been a Marine." I took that as a compliment.

Our trucks, which had been outside the gate all night, had to be inspected for booby traps. I don't think any three trucks have ever been inspected so thoroughly as ours were that morning. While I was talking with one of my guys, John, the other driver, Larry, got into his truck and started it up. "Well, he didn't blow up," I said. "Do you think it's safe for us to start up ours?"

"Thanks for letting me be the guinea pig," Larry said. We all were laughing now.

Later on I talked to a sergeant and a captain who were furious that our escorts hadn't brought us all the way to the gate the night before. They asked me for their names, but I wouldn't identify them. "This was my decision," I told them. "I will take responsibility for it. If anyone gets in trouble for this, it should be me." The escorts were a great group of guys—the same guys who had escorted my guys and me to TQ/Ridgeway the first time we made that trip. "If I had told them to take us all the way to the gate, they would've done it," I said. "But I told them they could leave us at the checkpoint."

After I talked with the captain, I realized that he wasn't as upset with the escorts as he was with the lieutenant who wouldn't let us inside the wire the night before. Later on, some of the troops told me that that lieutenant's ass was grass, and that we'd never again be left outside the wire at night. That was cool with me.

We got back to the business that brought us to the camp in the first place—delivering ice. The marines in Camp Fallujah were really nice and appreciative. I got the sense that they knew about what had happened to us and felt bad about it.

After a while, we were able to laugh about it. I kidded with my guys that we wouldn't need any escorts anymore, because, after all, we'd slept outside the wire in Fallujah. We were tough!

After returning to Anaconda after a mission, I walked into the reefer office and learned that Bob—the man nicknamed "Hard Head," who had sexually harassed me in Kuwait months earlier—was my new foreman. I had tried to file charges against him, and I knew he would be looking for revenge. Or he'd continue his harassment. Either way, I didn't want to deal with having him around. I immediately went to Ben, the new reefer supervisor. Privately I told him about my history with Bob, that I had tried to file charges against him but one of the bosses had decided that all Bob needed was a little talk, man to man.

"I can't work with Bob," I said, and I meant it. "One of us has to go. I know Bob is a foreman, so if somebody's got to go, it's going to be me. I don't care where you put me. I'll even go to tankers." That's how badly I wanted to get away from this creep.

Ben was no different from most guys when it comes to a woman's legitimate complaint about harassment. He didn't take it seriously.

"We're all adults here," he said. "I'll have a talk with Bob. You won't have any problems."

Ben said he needed all the capable people he could get his hands on, so he had no intention of transferring either one of us. "We're short on CCs," he said, "and I need all the good CCs I have right now."

In a way, of course, this was a compliment, and I chose to take it that way. I decided to keep my distance from Bob, but if I had to deal with him, I'd be polite and professional.

That attitude was not reciprocated. Bob almost immediately started messing with my convoys. On one occasion, he told me that my drivers had to line up in the convoy in the order they were listed on the mission sheet. I had a loud argument with Bob and then went over his head to Ben. "I place certain drivers in certain positions for a reason," I said. "It's based on what I know that they can handle." Ben agreed, so I won Round 1.

Sometime later, Bob decided he could tell me which one of my guys would be my driver, and which one would ride as my bobtail. The CC always made those decisions.

Only the CC knew who could handle those assignments. It's all about trust—the CC had to trust his or her driver, and the driver had to trust the CC if the shit hit the fan. And as far as I'm concerned, the bobtail driver has the most dangerous job in the convoy, riding at the end and being in charge of picking up drivers whose trucks get disabled in an attack.

Again, I went over Bob's head and went to Ben. We settled on a compromise: I got to pick my bobtail, while Bob decided who would be my driver. If this sounds like I gave in, I had my own little plan: I decided that if I couldn't pick my driver at the beginning of a mission, I sure as hell could pick my driver when things looked dangerous: I picked myself. I would drive on routes like the road from Anaconda to Scania, where hell often broke loose.

After all this time in Iraq, I knew I could trust myself.

In late June, Ed went back to the States for R&R and for a long talk with his wife. We hadn't seen much of each other because we were running on different convoys in different parts of the country. But often I'd find handwritten letters from him in the mail room in Anaconda. The letters were real, old-fashioned love letters.

One day in late June I ran into a woman, a fellow contractor, at a resort area that KBR leased out for its employees. I was with my guys, and we were just sort of passing some time while awaiting a new mission. The woman and I got to talking, and it turned out she had recently gotten married. She and her new husband had met in the Middle East, gotten engaged, and gone to Scotland to get married. Her husband had designed special rings for the ceremony and planned to surprise her with them. But somehow the rings got lost in Kuwait, and she never saw them. She had a tear in her eye as she talked about her husband's disappointment, about how much love had gone into those rings, and how much they meant to him.

Her story warmed my heart and made me think of Ed's letters, and the love and time that went into them. I told this woman, a complete stranger, all about Ed—that he loved me so much that he even considered my quirks beautiful, and that he noticed things about me that no man had ever noticed before.

For a few minutes, the two of us—complete strangers—were in our own world, a place where there was only love, a place far away from hatred and violence and war. As I talked about Ed, and this woman talked about her husband, we no longer were sitting in some mess hall in the Middle East. We were with the ones we loved, in spirit, and nobody else mattered.

The guys who worked with me, who knew me as a CC but not as a woman, were listening to this. I had completely forgotten about them. Eventually they seemed uncomfortable with all this girl talk and started making noises and smartass remarks. They had never seen this side of me, because on the job I had to be as tough as nails—and even tougher, because I didn't want them to think I was weak in any way. Their jokes and discomfort brought me back to reality, but I enjoyed every minute of the brief time I spent with another woman who understood the transforming power of love.

SEVEN

SUMMERS ARE ALWAYS LONG and hot in Iraq. The summer of 2004 was longer and hotter than most. The insurgents and terrorists continued to make life dangerous for our troops and for those of us who were trying to support them. Seven marines were killed during the first week in July in the Al-Anbar province. Four more of our troops, plus an Iraqi soldier, were killed when the insurgents fired mortar shells into a military headquarters in Samarra.

Every day brought news of more casualties from car bombs, mortar shells, roadside explosives—and executions. A number of foreign hostages were killed in cold blood. I reminded myself again that I would never be taken alive if I were ambushed.

At times like these, you find out who your friends are. The Filipinos announced that they would pull out of Iraq as quickly as possible. The Australians announced that they would increase their troop strength. As I was learning among my own peers in a much smaller setting, in wartime you need to know who you can depend on and who you can't. As a nation, we were learning that lesson in the summer of 2004.

Meanwhile, Saddam made his first appearance in court in Baghdad—one small step toward achieving justice for all the Iraqis he murdered during his reign. This was another victory for the good guys.

In mid-July, one of the KBR security guys in Anaconda told me that I was in trouble for something I posted on the website. I might be fired for it, he told me. I was shocked. He didn't know whether the trouble was with something I had posted on the website or on my discussion group, but he told me to shut it down.

I was concerned, and I went directly to the head of KBR security at Anaconda. I told him I had heard a rumor that I was in trouble because of something I posted online. The security chief pulled out a CD and put it in his computer. He had downloaded the website that Mary ran—not the Yahoo group. It turns out that I had pissed off some KBR people because I told the story about spending part of the night sleeping outside the wire in Fallujah. He told me I ought to shut down the website. "It would look better if you do it on your own," he said. And if I wanted to record what was going on in Iraq, I'd be better off just keeping an old-fashioned journal, rather than posting emails to my family. He said he didn't tell his own family what was going on in Iraq because he didn't want them to worry about him.

Well, that was fine for his family, but I told him I promised my family that they would get the truth about what was going on. Still, I took his point, and I called Mary and left a message asking her to take down the site. I then called my mother and asked her to keep calling

Mary until she actually spoke with her. She did, and Mary had the site down within half an hour.

Two days later, I was summoned to the Human Resources office at Anaconda. The head of HR himself wanted to talk to me about the website. I told him that my sister had taken the site down already, and I asked him if I would be fired because of this. "Some people want you fired," he said. But other people had stuck up for me, so I got off with a warning. He had me sign a paper showing that he had talked to me about the site and stating that I had Mary take it down. I don't know exactly what the problem was, but I think he was scared that the military would throw a fit.

Then he sort of lowered his voice and told me off the record that he didn't understand what the problem was. But, he added, KBR was scared that the military would throw a fit. My story, he said, was "embarrassing to the military."

For a while I made a point of being as vague as possible in my emails home, which really wasn't my style. But as I wrote to friends and family, "I want to make sure I am not giving anything away." I didn't want to lose my job.

I was working with a crew I really respected and liked, which made the drives through Iraq a lot less tense and anxious. Most of them had interesting and sometimes sad life stories, like one guy whose wife had left him while he was in Iraq. I worried about his mental state—he was devastated. Another guy, Larry, always wore shorts and flip-flops while on missions, instead of the jeans and steel-toed boots we were supposed to wear. Most of us, and I am guilty as well, did not wear our steel-toe boots. I had mine in the truck, in case safety caught me and said something about it, but I wore my Nikes. Still another guy, Tracey, always seemed to have a little alcohol in him, and, not surprisingly, usually was late for things. Greg, who was thirty something and married, spent a lot of time with me, just talking. One of my favorites was Roy, who was forty-three years old and was married with two kids. He had spent thirteen years in the Army before joining KBR. He was a terrific, happy person who was well liked.

There were others, too. I didn't get to know every-body really well, but I knew enough to know that I could trust them on a mission. You need to know that when you're in a war zone.

We were constantly on the move in July, which is the way we all preferred it. After a routine mission from Kuwait to Anaconda, I reported to the reefer office as usual to fill out my paperwork and see what our next assignment would be. The foreman on duty was my old "friend" Bob—better known as "Hard Head"—who bluntly told me that my crew would be going out the following morning, but not me. We had been told that crews would be kept together as often as possible, and my crew in particular was doing a great job. We showed what you can achieve through teamwork and trust.

I let Hard Head know exactly how I felt, but he had a clever answer. The crew, he explained, actually was staying together. They simply were getting a new CC. Besides, he said, convoy commanders were supposed to rotate between driving and office work. Company policy, you see. It was time for me to learn how to do some office work.

I already knew what went on in the office. I had helped other supervisors with various jobs long before Bob became my foreman. I had even turned down an administration job in reefers because I wanted to keep running missions. I didn't need this crap.

I also knew that if I refused to go along with Hard Head's scheme, I could wind up in a lot of trouble. So I kept my temper and told him, "Well, this is my job. I don't like it, my guys won't like it, but if I have to do it, I will." I wasn't about to give him a reason to fire me. But I told him that I wanted to tell my guys what was going on. Not him. Me. He agreed.

I got on my radio and told the guys to meet me in front of my truck. I don't know what they were expecting, but when they got there, I told them I was being rotated into the office, and they would be getting a new CC. I was right: They didn't like it. They asked who would be their new CC, a perfectly legitimate question. Hard Head had told me, but I had forgotten, so I called him on the radio and asked. When he replied with the new CC's name, my guys let out groans. Their new CC had a pretty bad reputation. The guys told me they wanted to talk to Hard Head personally. I relayed this information to Hard Head, and he grudgingly agreed to meet with them.

He arrived in a pickup truck, and with a scowl made it clear that he wasn't particularly happy with this turn of events. "If you guys don't like this, you can go home," he said. My guys didn't take the bait. Larry calmly explained that they wanted me to know how much they appreciated and respected me, and that they would rather keep running with me. "Well," said Hard Head, "if you want her that bad, you can have her." He got back in his pickup and took off.

We were surprised, because we didn't expect him to back down, and happy, because we'd be staying together. Privately I wondered why Hard Head gave in so quickly. I went to the office and asked him to his face. He said he and our supervisor, Ben, were worried that I'd take my complaints to KBR's operations manager. To avoid that, he said, they decided to let me have my way.

I didn't ask any more questions, because I had my

crew, and that's all I cared about. Still, I wondered if Hard Head was worried about my bringing up the sexual harassment charges against him, or if Ben was worried that he'd get in trouble for not transferring one of us, Hard Head or me, when I told him about the problem between us.

The following night we were on the road back to Kuwait, driving a route I had traveled many times before. It was the normal fifteen-truck convoy. We would deadhead (run empty) from Anaconda to Kuwait, pick up loaded ice trailers, and go back to Anaconda.

Everything seemed routine as we drove south of Baghdad, through nondescript landscapes. I was driving, although I had a driver, a guy named Robert, who was new to the job. Hard Head made me take him as my driver, but I wasn't about to let a rookie drive me. As usual, because I was the CC, we drove in the front of the convoy.

You're never really at ease on these missions—you're in a war zone, after all. Still, I was stunned to hear Greg's frantic voice on the radio. "I'm taking fire," he said. He was behind me. I grabbed my radio.

"What direction?" I asked. I couldn't hear or see anything.

Then Larry reported that he was taking fire, too. Then a couple more guys. Now I could see flashes of gunfire in the mirror, bright, angry orange lights against the dark desert sky. We were under attack. We were being ambushed, and it was all taking place in my rearview mirror.

My guys were getting shot at, and I could do nothing to help them. I couldn't stop. I had to keep moving.

Then I heard another familiar voice. It was my friend Roy: "I've been hit!" he said. I could hear the pain in his voice. I had no idea where he had been shot or if the wound was life-threatening. I got on the radio again and told my bobtail driver, Tim, to be ready to pick up Roy if he couldn't keep driving. Roy's voice came over the air again.

"I've been hit."

Gunfire flashed in the mirror, followed by the flash of a mortar hit. The radio was alive with voices—most of them calm and professional, but, given the circumstances, there was a lot of tension in those voices, too.

I kept my eyes on the road while I replied to Roy.

"I know, hon," I said. I couldn't help myself with the "hon" bit. It came out naturally. "But we have to get ya'll to a safe zone before we can stop." I had to keep him moving. It was always better if an injured driver could drive himself to a safe area. That kept us from having to leave a truck behind, and kept the bobtail driver from having to get out of his truck and risk his life by picking up the injured guy.

I knew we were approaching a U.S. military checkpoint, thank God. I kept talking to Roy. I had to keep him conscious. He told me he was in a lot of pain.

"I know, Roy," I said. "But you have to drive that truck. We can't stop for you until we get you in the checkpoint. The guys behind you are counting on you." That was the truth. If Roy stopped, the guys behind him would be trapped. We had to keep Roy moving, just for a few more miles, just for a few more minutes. The checkpoint was just ahead, somewhere in the darkness. "C'mon Roy, you can do it. I have faith in you. I know it hurts, but you can do it."

Finally, the lead escort got to the checkpoint and stopped to check in with the troops. I was fighting the urge to shove that lead escort out of the way so all of us could get past the checkpoint and into a safe area. I had no idea whether the guys farther back in the convoy were still in what we called the "kill zone."

Roy was hurting big time, but he still was driving. Finally we pulled into and through the checkpoint. I got on the radio and told my guys to stay in their trucks. Then I grabbed my helmet, jumped out of my truck, and made a mad dash to Roy's truck. I got there just as Ben, who was driving behind Roy, and two soldiers were getting him out.

He had been shot in the right leg, just below the knee. Luckily, the wound was not life-threatening, but he had lost a fair amount of blood. Ben and the two soldiers laid him on the asphalt road. The medic cut his jeans past his knee and started bandaging the wound, which looked like bloody raw meat. Both the entry and exit wounds were a little bigger than a half-dollar coin. I focused on Roy's face, and his eyes, trying to keep his attention on something other than his leg. The medic told me that the wound wasn't too bad, and that Roy would be all right. They hit him with morphine.

"You did a great job," I said to Roy. "You're going to be okay."

It was a relief to realize that Roy was going to make it. Now I had to worry about other things, like Roy's truck. He obviously wasn't going to be able to finish the drive back to Kuwait, but I didn't want to leave it behind at the checkpoint. So I asked my guys to see if we could get it moving. They discovered that one of the truck's steer tires was losing air—it had taken a bullet. What's strange is that I never heard the air coming out of the tire until they found the hole. When I was told about the leak, I could hear it plainly. That's how focused I was on Roy.

The guys got right on it, changing the tire and then checking the truck for any other damage. The whole time, they were talking to Roy as he lay nearby. The troops ordered a chopper to get him to a hospital ASAP.

I had three things going on at once. I had to make sure Roy was taken care of, I had to assess the damage to his truck, and I had to report the ambush to KBR over our Qualcomm system. I asked my driver to handle that, but the guy didn't know how to run the Qualcomm— thank you again, Hard Head, for sticking me with a rookie. So I asked Ben to handle it, and he did a great job communicating everything to headquarters while I sat with Roy, holding his hand and telling him everything would be fine.

Everybody did his job. Everything worked like clockwork. You'd have thought that we'd rehearsed this scenario a hundred times. I had been running with a couple of the guys for five weeks, and most of the others for three weeks. You get to know people mighty quickly in a war zone. I had told them when I first ran with them: We had to be able to trust each other with our lives. We had to know we could depend on each other.

As the chopper landed to pick up Roy, kicking up sand and blasting us with noise, the guys came around the truck one by one to say good-bye and wish him the best. He told us that he'd be back so that he and Ben could whip Greg and me at a game of spades.

As the chopper lifted off, the military told us that we had to get moving again. Another convoy was behind us and closing in. We had to clear out to make room for them.

As I walked back to my truck, the escort unit's sergeant took me aside.

"How are *we* doing?" he asked. He clearly was concerned about how we were holding up. I appreciated that concern.

"This is the first time I've had one of my guys hurt," I said.

He looked at me and replied: "This is a first for me, too." I assured him that we were okay. I think he was, too.

I asked my driver if he'd take over Roy's truck, and I'd drive myself. Even with Roy's blood on the floor of the truck and the passenger window blown out from the bullet, he agreed without hesitation. He wasn't so bad after all, for a rookie. We got back in our trucks and got moving again.

We weren't on the road very long when our escorts told us to stop and turn off our lights. There was another ambush under way just ahead of us—a northbound convoy was coming under attack. My heart sank. We just sat there on the road, waiting. We could hear nothing—it was completely quiet. I usually keep my windows down a little during a night mission, so I can use my ears as well as my eyes. Now I rolled them down a little more. Nothing.

It was dark, too. The only light we could see was coming from houses off in the distance. I said a silent prayer for my guys: "Please don't let anything more happen to these guys tonight. They've been through enough. They don't need this."

In the distance, I saw the power grid in front of us go dark.

"Oh, shit." I went from prayer to profanity in a second. I knew, we all knew, that when the terrorists set up an ambush at night, they have somebody watching us a short distance from the enemy position. Then they cut the power lines to let the ambush team know that we were approaching.

Then the power grid behind us went dark, too. "Oh, shit," I said again, but louder.

No sounds. Not even the crackle of somebody's radio. After forty-five minutes of utter anxiety, the escorts got on the radio and said it was okay to get moving again. I told my guys to keep their eyes open during the drive, and to stay as quiet as possible.

We kept moving in the darkness. The only sound I heard, other than the rumble of the trucks, was my own voice, reminding me that I had to hold it together.

After about ninety minutes, we pulled into a checkpoint at Scania. We were safe. I couldn't help myself—I started to cry. I let myself go because I could. I still was in my truck, so nobody could see me. But once we got to the gate, I dried my tears. "Don't let them see you cry-ing," I said to myself.

The stress and the anxiety had gotten to me, but more than anything else, I was concerned about Roy. I knew it wasn't my fault that he got hurt, but still—he was my guy, he was in my convoy. During the last leg of the drive, I re-played the ambush over and over again in my mind. Could I have done more? Should I have handled anything differently? It had been an awful night in Iraq.

The guys and I did our best to calm each other's nerves. There would be paperwork to file and reports to write about the attack, but that would be done in the morning. For now, we just talked among ourselves and looked over Roy's shot-up truck.

One of my guys told me that the escorts in the middle of the convoy and at the end did not return fire during the ambush. I thought that was strange.

I told them to get some rest, and I'd do the same. As I climbed back into my truck, I realized how much worse the night could have been.

I needed to talk to somebody, somebody who didn't need to see a brave face.

I called Ed, who was still on his R&R in the States. He didn't pick up. So I called Jack, my ex.

Jack told me I did a good job and now it was time for me to get off the road. I knew he would say that. Jack himself had gotten off the road. But I told Jack I had no desire, even now, to get off the road. I loved running missions. I wasn't about to be frightened away from doing my job.

I finally got to sleep. The following morning was devoted to the paperwork and reports that come with being attacked. I had to give a statement. So did my guys. We were told that there was a combat stress team available if we needed to talk. I thought that might be a good idea, until it was over and I realized that my guys were more angry after their session with the team than they were before it. It was just really sinking in that some of the escorts didn't return fire. What the hell was that about?

A week or so later, I had the same escorts for a mission out of Anaconda. The sergeant who had taken me aside after the attack approached me again and asked after Roy, a nice gesture. I told him what I had heard— Roy was giving his nurses hell and was dying to get back on the road. I then had a question for him: Was it true, as my guys told me, that his troops didn't return fire during the ambush?

It was, he said, but for a reason: A northbound convoy was passing on the other side of the road during the assault, and the end of that convoy was in the troops' line of fire. The soldiers couldn't return fire without hitting the other convoy. It's funny, but I had no memory, until now, of that northbound convoy. Neither did my guys. We were completely focused on Roy and on getting out of the kill zone as quickly as we could.

We found the bullet that hit Roy. It had gone through the driver's door, through his leg, and was lodged in the passenger door of his truck. I kept the bullet and promised to send it to Roy.

When the mission was over and we were back in Kuwait, I heard from friends that people were talking about the ambush and about how I did. One of the comments reported back to me was this: "She did a good job holding it together even though she's a woman." On the surface, I let it go. But I didn't forget it.

Once we were back in Kuwait, one of the KBR bosses, a guy named Ken, told me that he was going to split up my crew and send us in different directions to get reloaded. I was furious. First of all, I thought somebody from KBR should have had the decency to tell my guys what a good job they did during the mission when Roy was shot. These guys had been total pros. They deserved a pat on the back and a day off.

Ken disagreed. He said that the company shouldn't

"baby" my guys just because they had been through a tough mission. He said we needed to keep moving ice up north—there was no time for nonsense like a day off and a word of thanks.

I told Ken that it was pretty clear to me that KBR didn't give a damn about my guys. They had spent weeks on the roads, running back-to-back missions; they got shot at; they saw one of their crew get hurt—all I was asking for was a day off.

No, the bosses said. We had to get back on the road—it was July, they said, and the troops needed ice in northern Iraq. When I kept sticking up for my guys, they played the assault card: They knew I was scheduled to give a statement to the Kuwaitis about the night I was attacked, so they used that against me. "You're too stressed out," they said. "You really ought to hand your crew over to somebody else."

This was unbelievable. They kept at it, preying on my insecurities. "You really have to take care of this other problem," they said. They said I ought to talk to a counselor. The truth is, they weren't wrong.

In the end, I relented, but mainly because they offered to have Ed take my guys back north to Anaconda. If I couldn't bring them back "home"—and that's how we thought of Anaconda after spending so much time there—having Ed as CC was the next best thing.

I felt I ought to tell the guys myself that I wouldn't be

with them on the trip back north, and why. None of them knew about the attack, although some of them had heard rumors about it. I told them what had happened, and that I needed to talk to the Kuwaiti authorities and a counselor. They all said they understood, and that I had their full support.

Just before we separated, the guys told me that if I saw the guy who attacked me, I should let them know and they'd take care of him. I appreciated the sentiments.

When they got to Anaconda, my guys were split up and assigned to different crews. Chopped up and thrown to the four winds—for no good reason, as far as I could tell.

While I was in Kuwait, I spoke with lawyers and with a counselor named David Nix, who had worked with Tommy Hamill's family after he was kidnapped earlier in the year. I liked Dave and met with him every day that I was in Kuwait—he was a great help to me. Not only did we talk about the attack, we talked about the ambushes I had been through. I said that KBR had nobody to take care of my guys after the ambush.

Dave said he had never had to deal with a rape victim before and made several calls to the States to speak with other counselors with more experience in rape cases. At one point, he told me to write about the attack, put it into words, let it out.

When it came time to meet with the Kuwaiti authorities, Dave was by my side. I wanted Ed with me, but he had been transferred to flatbeds and wasn't running missions to Kuwait. Ed had been with me every step of the way as I tried to come to terms with what had happened to me, so I was upset that he couldn't be with me this time, too. But I did bring with me a coin Ed had given me, with a rendering of the World Trade Center on one side and the Pentagon on the other. It was a reminder to me of why I was in Iraq, and why I couldn't let this rapist stop me from doing my job.

Dave turned out to be a wonderful source of strength in Ed's absence. When I showed up to give my statement to the Kuwaitis, there were more people on hand than I anticipated. I thought it would be just myself, Dave, an interpreter, and the Kuwaiti prosecutor. But KBR had sent a lawyer, and the Kuwaitis had three other people with them in addition to the prosecutor. I felt uncomfortable telling my story to so many people, especially with only one other woman—the interpreter—in the room.

It wasn't easy. There were lots of questions. The Kuwaitis asked me to relive the attack in every painful detail. At several points, I didn't think I could go on. Dave helped keep me going—at one point he told me that if I could get through the ambushes and nearly getting killed by my ex-husband, I could make it through this. The whole time I had that coin in my hand, and I was squeezing it so hard that my hand was bruised by the time the questions were over.

But I got through it.

On August 18, I sent a long email back home. A year earlier, I had started on a journey that took me to a place I could not have imagined, doing things I never thought I was capable of, under conditions I had never experienced. To my friends and family, I wrote:

> It was one year ago today that I kissed my three boys good-bye, hopped on the back of my dad's motorcycle, and made the drive to Memphis to catch a plane to Houston. In some ways, it doesn't seem like it has been that long, but in others, it feels like longer. I still have five

weeks until my year [in Iraq] is up. I have mixed emotions about it all. Happy, sad, confused, scared, and ready for more.

I know that I have changed a bit since I went to Houston and even more since I got over here. When I left the States to do this, I had all the "right" reasons in my head for doing it. I wanted to support our troops . . . I know that in some ways I had a romanticized idea of what I would be doing, but I also knew that I would be going into a war zone.

I know that I have said that I believe in what we are doing there and why we are here. I have seen the [Iraqis'] lives change over the last year, some for the better, some for the worse. That is the way of war. And yes, it is still a war. The media and our government can say that the "war" is over, but in reality, it is not. It is still going strong.

But also it has been a road of discovery. When I stepped on that plane, I hoped that I could leave all my problems behind and start over. Yes, I know it sounds like a very wild way to start your life over, but when have I done things like everyone else? I knew that I would find out who I am and what I am made of. I believe that I have done some of that. We never truly know who we are and how we will react to things until we are put in that situation. Honor, integrity, pride, and humanity can all be rediscovered.

I know more about me, I know more about the world we live in. I have seen man's inhumanity to man, as well as man's love and understanding of man. I have also found that I have places in my heart that are cold and uncaring, as well as the uncontrollable places that are full of warmth and love.

So my story of being over here is not just one of a female truck driver driving in a war zone in Iraq. It is a story of me finding the world, and of me finding me. And this is just the beginning.

It was late August, and my mind was drifting a little bit. I was due for some R&R in about a month, and I was planning to get on a plane and disappear into the rain forest in Malaysia for a week or so. After a year in the desert, I figured a rain forest would be a nice change of pace!

Insurgent attacks and just plain bad luck continued to plague our convoys. I was involved in a couple of minor ambushes and in a scary pileup on a sand-covered road. As each truck kicked up more and more sand, visibility got worse and worse. We were riding blind, and as a result, several vehicles plowed into each other. A couple of guys were hurt, but nobody was killed. One of our trucks caught fire. All in all, we were lucky. As I mentioned in an email home, "I woke up breathing and didn't get shot at today, so it is a good day."

On the night of August 21, I was part of a convoy headed from Kuwait to Anaconda, on a road on the east side of Baghdad code-named Irish. It was considered a dangerous route, a four-lane highway always busy with civilian traffic—even at night. The road passed through a marketplace, although for the most part it was lined with houses.

I had a driver with me, another guy named Robert, but I got behind the wheel when we hit a stretch of road that took us through Baghdad, from Scania to Anaconda. I was pretty familiar with the road, having driven it many times before. Robert was a capable guy, but he understood my policy of driving myself through this stretch of road. This wasn't the way KBR wanted it done—the bosses wanted the driver behind the wheel at all times, with the CC in the passenger seat. But I thought it was best if I got behind the wheel.

I was chatting about routine stuff with my driver when, out of nowhere, I saw a flash of light as we approached an overpass. A split second later, Bob was yelling that he was hit. He took a bullet in his right knee. He was in a lot of pain, but the wound wasn't too bad—the bullet hit the truck first.

Then the sky lit up with flares, tracer fire, mortar fire, and explosives. We were not just taking fire—we had driven right into a full-blown ambush, and the bad guys had some heavy-duty firepower.

Of course, we had to keep moving. Stop, and we were dead. So I kept my foot down on the pedal.

I had an escort in front of me. They were not yet returning fire, because under the rules of engagement, they had to have positive identification of the enemy before they could fire back. This restriction was a constant source of frustration for the troops.

I immediately got on the radio and told my guys that we were taking fire. As I did, I saw another flash and felt a burning sensation in the back of my right arm. I knew I was hit, but I also knew it wasn't too bad. I had the wheel in one hand and my radio in the other. "I'm taking fire from the front, the left and the right," I said.

I turned to Bob. "How bad is it?"

"Not too bad, but it hurts," he said.

Shit.

"Put some pressure on it," I said. I figured that would

help stop the bleeding. "We have to get through this kill zone."

My bobtail behind me radioed that one of the TCNs in the convoy was hit in the leg. He got then out of his truck. Damn it.

"Pick him up and move out," I told my bobtail.

The TCN stopped his truck in the middle of the road, so now there was a lot of separation in the convoy. That's not good—you don't want them to be able to pick you apart in pieces. I stayed in radio contact with them. My bobtail got out of his truck and directed the rest of the convoy around the TCN's truck while the wounded TCN got into my bobtail's truck. They were still taking fire.

The rest of us stopped for a while, but when we heard the rear of the convoy was still taking fire, we got moving again. All the while, I could hear what was going on behind me over the radio. Once we were out of the kill zone, we stopped and waited for the rest of the convoy.

While we were stopped, I grabbed a first aid kit, crawled across the truck's doghouse, which is the hump between the seats, and tried to apply a pressure bandage to my driver's wound. I couldn't cut his jeans from that position, so I crawled back, got out of the truck, ran over to the passenger side, opened that door, stood on the steps, and started putting the bandage on. One of the troops from the lead escort was watching my back.

While I was getting the bandage in place, we heard the *pop-pop-pop* of small-arms fire. We were under attack again.

Robert yelled at me: "Get back in the truck!" The escort behind me opened fire at the unseen snipers. There is nothing quite as sweet as the sound of gunfire when you know it's coming from a soldier who is covering your tail.

"Tie off the bandage," I told my driver. Then I scrambled back to the driver's side, pulled myself back into the truck, and got on the radio to alert the rest of the convoy that we were taking fire, again. Then I got rolling.

Next to me, Robert was praying out loud. I got on the radio and told the guys to follow me. Ahead of us, I could see a goddamn traffic jam. There was no way I could stop. We'd be sitting ducks. I'd have to bust through the traffic so we could get through. "I'm making a hole," I said over the radio. "Follow me."

Ahead of me was the first car blocking our way. I looked down and saw the faces of two children in the backseat. I couldn't just ram this car. So I tried my best to sideswipe it, to push it out of the way as gently as possible. I forced the vision of those two kids out of my head as I approached the next car in my way. This time, I didn't look down into the car's windows. I just kept going, ramming the car out of my way. I don't remember feeling the blow as my truck hit the car.

I hit a total of four cars, and tore the hell out of the right side of my truck. The military vehicle behind me hit more cars as they widened the path for the convoy.

"Drive like you stole it," I told my guys via radio. "It's not your truck. It's KBR's. They can buy a new one."

I was in front because our lead escort had moved to the back to cover our tails. I was the leader of this convoy. It was up to me to get us through this ambush and into safety.

We took heavy fire for about three or four miles, and intermittent fire for another fifteen miles. Our escorts were great—they returned the fire and gave us plenty of cover as we drove toward Camp Taji to get help for our wounded—Bob, the TCN who had to be picked up, and a soldier who took some glass in his face.

In the past, I'd watched ambushes through the rearview mirror. This was the first time I took fire myself. Usually they hit the middle or the end of a convoy, not the front, where I normally was as the CC. And while I've had my guys get hurt, like Roy, it's very different when the wounded guy is sitting in the same truck. When Roy was hit, I could hear the fear and pain. With Bob sitting right next to me, I could see it as well. As for myself, I had a little shrapnel in my right arm.

On the ride to Taji, I kept my truck at about seventy kilometers per hour, which was slow, but I didn't want to lose the rear of the convoy. At one point, one of the military vehicles behind me asked me to slow down so they could get out in front of me. "I know where I'm going," I replied. They wanted to cover me, they said, so I slowed down and let the Humvee take the lead.

We finally pulled through the gate and off to the side in the first wide area we could find. I jumped out and ran around to Bob's side of the truck. The cab's steps were gone—I lost them while bashing my way through traffic. I asked two soldiers to give me a hand getting Bob out of the truck. They helped get him to the ground. Medics and ambulances were on the spot quickly.

One of the medics kept calling me on the radio, asking me to let them have a look at my arm. I told him to take care of my guys. "I've had scratches worse than this," I said. I had to make sure my guys were okay. Then I had to check out the trucks to see if they were fit to finish the trip to Anaconda. Meanwhile, my Qualcomm was going off like crazy—the bosses were looking for more information about the ambush. Who was hurt? How bad? Could the trucks continue? Did we want to go ahead with the mission? I didn't have time for the medics, although I saw one eventually. He told me there was nothing much he could do, that the metal fragments would work their way out through my skin.

After everything calmed down a bit and I was sitting in my truck looking it over, I noticed that my cooler, which was sitting on the doghouse, had two bullet holes in it. I stuck my head out of the truck and yelled to the sergeant who was part of my escort unit. "Hey, sarge, I hope you got those bastards. They shot up my cooler."

The sergeant laughed, and so did the other guys who heard it. Everybody seemed to relax a bit, which was my intention.

But once I had time to think about what had gone down, I realized that it should have been me who caught that bullet, not Bob. I was supposed to be in the passenger seat, and Bob was supposed to be driving, according to KBR policy. Talk about guilt. I felt terrible and told another driver, who gave me a hug and reassured me. He also said he'd be happy to be my driver anytime, which made me feel a bit better.

We had to keep pushing on to Anaconda, and I had to decide whether or not my truck could make the trip. The bullet that hit Bob had also hit the upper part of the cooling system of the truck. I had lost some antifreeze, but the engine was staying within an acceptable temperature range, so I decided that I was going to drive the truck to Anaconda. I didn't want to leave a much-needed load of ice going to waste in Taji, where it wasn't needed.

As we made our way to Anaconda, the truck heated up. At one point the gauge read 255 degrees. I told the escorts that we either needed to slow down or speed up. I needed to keep the rpms at 1,500 to keep the truck cooled down. They told me that I could set the pace and they would stay with me. When we got to the south gate of Anaconda, we had to wait an hour to proceed into the camp because of a broken-down tanker truck. Two of the soldiers from the lead Humvee walked back to my truck. I rolled my window down to talk to them.

"We want to thank you," they said.

I was puzzled, to say the least. "Thank me for what?"

They explained that each of them had made twenty dollars thanks to me. Some of the other troops didn't think I'd make it to Anaconda with my shot-up truck. These two soldiers said I would, and they had put their money on it.

Once inside the wire, I radioed the reefer office and told them that we were home and that I needed to speak with people from the Safety office. Two Safety guys took pictures of my truck and asked me questions. I told them that I would have a statement for them in the morning, but not now. I was tired, and so were my guys. They were cool with that. But the lead person on duty that night for reefers told me that my crew and I had to get the ice loaded onto other trailers before we could go to bed. Here we had been ambushed, left two injured drivers at

Taji, and all they could think about was getting the ice moved! Although there was a counselor in the camp, as there always was, nobody had notified her that we were in camp. My foreman had been led to believe we were headed for another camp, and so he was unprepared when we rolled into Anaconda.

It didn't matter. We had to move the ice. While we were getting that job done, other reefer convoys came in. They had heard about the ambush, and they wanted to know more details. Talking with them helped me deal with it.

Finally, after we moved the ice and I sent the guys to bed, I called the States. I talked to my stepdad and told him what had happened. Then I went to bed.

The following morning, I showed up at the reefer office at nine o'clock, expecting to talk to my foreman about the ambush. Instead, he told me that my crew and I would be going out again that night.

I hit the roof. The guys had told me they didn't want to go out that night, and I had promised them that they wouldn't have to. It was a bad ambush, I told my foreman, one of the worst on any KBR convoy. He countered by telling me that he was short of CCs. I told him that if need be, I would go, but the guys deserved a day off. He agreed to that, and I got a new crew. We hooked to trailers and staged, but we didn't go out that night because of a shortage of escorts. We went out the next night instead, on what turned out to be an uneventful trip.

While I was getting that convoy together, I ran into a friend of mine from Cedar, a guy who went by the call sign Tiger Six. He had heard that I was injured in an ambush, and he asked to take a look at my arm. We saw five wounds that were festering on the back of my arm. I asked him to help me pop out the metal under the skin. We got four of the five shards. The fifth was too deep and Tiger Six didn't want to dig into my arm that much. I told him to just get it out. He tried but ended up leaving the bit of shrapnel in there.

In the days that followed, a number of guys asked me if I thought this attack was a sign that I ought to get out of reefers and take a safer job. I have to admit that a part of me wanted to. But in the end I knew I couldn't just run and hide. I couldn't let the sons of bitches win. I talked to a friend about this, and he put it to me this way: It's the mother, daughter, or sister who says Yes, it's time to find a job behind the wire. It's the American in you that says No, I'm not going to let the bad guys win. People like me and my crew, he said, along with our Army escorts, make up the American spirit.

I couldn't have agreed more.

A few days after the ambush, I got online in Cedar and learned that I had about two hundred emails from friends and family offering support and prayers. They had heard about the ambush through my mother, who had posted something on my Yahoo discussion group site after I called my stepdad.

The wife of a truck driver based at BIAP and a driver herself sent a message, saying, "As a woman truck driver, I must say—GOOD JOB! You did us proud by handling the situation. All the best on a quick recovery."

Everybody wanted to know more details, so I posted a long account of the attack on the discussion group. I made a point of thanking our escorts, who had really saved the day. I mentioned the unit by name. Here's what I wrote:

On August 21 we were ambushed
again. My driver, who was shot in the leg,

is going good. A TCN driver was also shot and I have no news on him. One soldier got glass in the face, was treated, and carried on with the convoy. I got small pieces of shrapnel in the back of my right arm. It is really nothing. I want to give my thanks to the 1st of the 86th FA for doing such a great job in covering our tails as we made our getaway. I want to give my personal thanks for the soldier that stood at my back and covered me as I bandaged my driver's knee. You guys are great!

I meant every word of it. Our escorts were fabulous. As far as I was concerned, they saved our lives. I wrote a commendation report for the unit. A sergeant major said he was delighted to get it, because most of the reports he got were complaints. He told me he would try to find the name of the soldier who had watched my back while I tended to Bob. These guys deserved some recognition for the job they did. So did my bobtail, who risked his life to pick up the injured TCN.

The following morning, we were scheduled to leave Cedar and push on south, but the insurgents blew up some oil pipelines that ran under the road we were supposed to take. So our drive was postponed.

I spent the afternoon at the PX, parking my bobtail in

a place nearby. When I came out of the PX, my truck was gone. That was strange. I went immediately to the camp supervisor, a guy named Fletcher, who had been nice to me in the past. He said he had been looking for me, and he took me to the security office.

I didn't know what the hell was going on. The security guys asked me about the Yahoo group site. "Yes, I have one," I said. "What's the problem?"

They handed me a sheet of paper. It was a printout of the front page of the group site, with my message thanking my escorts.

They told me I was fired.

I was stunned. They said I had violated security by mentioning the unit number of my escorts.

I tried to argue with them, hoping that somehow I could change their minds. Shit, I still had shrapnel in my arm, and now I'm getting fired?

They told me I would not be allowed to go back to Anaconda for my belongings—I would be sent south to Kuwait with another convoy the following morning. (Ed eventually mailed my stuff home to me.) I'd have to go as a rider. And I was not to tell anybody why I was fired.

I went straight to my friend Tiger Six. I told him that I had just been fired. I was devastated. Finally, after all I had been through in my life, I had found something I was meant to do. And I loved it. What was I going to do now?

I called Ed on the satellite phone and told him. He was

furious. It made no sense, except if you believe that some KBR people were gunning for me and looking for the smallest excuse to fire me. That's what I believed. They failed me on security at the Safir, where I was assaulted, and now they were firing me for security reasons? Nice irony.

One thing you could say about KBR: They were pretty damn efficient when they wanted to get rid of you. They wanted to put me on a plane to Germany a day after they let me go. I talked them into giving me some time to find another job, but I couldn't. So, in a matter of days, I went from being a CC with shrapnel in her arm to an out-of-work truck driver who had allegedly violated military security.

Even as I tried to make sense of this, Ed was recovering from an ear injury he suffered when his convoy was hit by an IED in late August. And he had lost his passport. So much for our plans to spend R&R in Malaysia. The attack and my firing seemed to get Ed thinking about the future and where I would fit in. He said he was going to confront his wife once and for all. I prepared myself for the worst.

Although I was fired, I still felt responsible for the guys who'd traveled the roads of Iraq with me. Before flying home from Kuwait, I went to the KBR Safety office to see if anybody had news about my TCN driver, had been shot a few days earlier.

The Safety people told me that the driver had been taken to a local hospital, but that he called his company from the hospital to report that he was receiving death threats. He then "escaped" from the hospital and called his office again from somewhere in Iraq—but nobody was sure where. Because he was not a KBR employee, the Safety office didn't know the driver's name, passport number, or anything else about him. They needed this information to help find him. I gave them the mission log with all the information they would need to track him down. Later, while en route home, I received an email telling me that they had found him. He was OK, and he thanked me for my concern.

I got home to the States in mid-October, just in time to commemorate the first anniversary of my deployment to Kuwait and Iraq. Having some time to myself gave me a chance to think about how much I had changed, and how much was left undone. I still regarded this part of my life as the beginning, not the ending, of something new and different.

On my website, I wrote:

> I look back at the last year and am a bit amazed at all that I have done and seen. For a kid who grew up in Arkansas and became a truck driver, what I have done this year is beyond anything I thought I would ever do . . . Until September last year, the only time I had ever left the U.S. was to deliver freight into Canada. So flying halfway around the world to drive a truck is simply amazing. Then, to think that it was in a war zone with bullets and explosives, and was voluntary, well, I sometimes wonder what the hell I was thinking. But ya know, I wouldn't trade any of it. It has been a great year. I have been through quite a bit . . . I have been from Kuwait to Mosul and out to Fallujah, and into a few camps

that are no longer there. I have seen the City of Ur and I have seen the bombs left by the Iraqi Army sitting on the ground. I have met children who are trying to hustle you for anything they can get. And I have seen those same children become kids again after a while . . . I have seen women hit in the street because they did something that their husbands didn't like. And I have seen the eyes of the little girls and women widen to see a woman driving a truck. I once was asked if I was preaching to the women . . . doing my part to liberate their minds. My answer was that I didn't have to. All I had to do was drive my truck. Seeing a woman driving a truck was enough to put the thought into their heads that women are good for more than making babies and domestic duties. You don't have to preach your ideas. You just have to live them.

That's what I did for almost a year—I tried to live my ideas. I tried to see who I was and what I could become. And while I came home earlier than I wanted to, I saw more than a glimpse of the person I was determined to become.

That glimpse was enough to convince me that I could reach this promised land. Getting fired, I decided, was just another stumbling block. A year earlier, it would have been insurmountable. But now, I looked at it as just another challenge to overcome.

The sudden and unwanted adjustment to civilian life wasn't easy. I missed the guys and I missed the life. I missed that feeling we all had of trust in each other. Race didn't matter. Religion didn't matter. It didn't matter whether or not you liked the person in the truck behind you. We were all brothers and sisters on those convoys. I missed Ed, too. We saw each other briefly when he came home for R&R, and then he was fired, too. We talked a lot, but then the phone calls stopped coming. The dumping of Cindy had begun.

I was proud to say that I was a civilian contractor in Iraq. I was proud to say that my son was a soldier. I was proud to be an American. And I was proud of the work we were doing in Iraq.

And I was proud of myself. It was a nice feeling, for a change.

For my oldest son, Kenny, duty called on December 15. He phoned me from Fort Hood, Texas, to say he was leaving for Iraq in a few hours. Although I had prepared myself for this moment, I broke down anyway. Through my tears, I told him to be careful and that I loved him. Just like millions of moms have said to their soldier sons through the years.

He told me that if I ever made contact with the unit that escorted us during that ambush, he wanted to pass along a message of his own: "From one soldier to another, thank you for covering my mom's ass."

I was lucky enough to pass on those thanks, and my own, via email in early 2005.

By then, I was getting ready to prove that all of this really was just the beginning—the beginning of my commitment to my buddies, to my country, to my soldier son and his buddies, and to myself.

EIGHT

BEFORE KENNY LEFT FOR IRAQ, he made me promise him that I wouldn't look for work over there myself. He said, while he was training in Fort Hood, "I need to be thinking about me and my buddies. I don't want to be worrying about you being out on the roads and getting shot at."

I had to respect my son's request, although I didn't like it. He was the soldier; he would be carrying a gun in a war zone. He needed to be focused on his assignment. He didn't need a distraction that might put him or his buddies in harm's way—any more, that is, than they already were.

So I took a job driving in the States.

I wish I could say that after my time overseas, after all that I learned about myself and about the world we live in, I was at peace. I wish I could say I was content. I wish I could say that I had made an easy transition to my old life.

None of that, however, was true. While I understood that I was not the person I was before I flew to Kuwait, it was for that very reason that I had a hard time adjusting to what you might call "normal" life. I missed my buddies, I missed the troops, and, truth be told, I missed the action.

But I had made a promise to my soldier son, and I had every intention of honoring that promise.

In early December, I was on Interstate 84 on Baker Hill in Oregon when I got stuck on the road in a snowstorm. Ahead of me, a truck carrying new cars—we call them "parking lots"—had jackknifed on the icy highway, and two trucks had piled into it. Traffic came to a halt. I didn't move for three hours.

For those hours, it was just me, the truck, the snow, and the sound of other drivers over the radio. They were bitching about the weather, the delay, and everything else. A year and a half earlier, I might have joined in the complaining. It was a pain, after all, to be stuck on a snowy highway in the middle of Oregon.

But that would have been the old me. Now I looked outside and thought to myself: I love seeing snow. What are they complaining about? Seeing snow means I'm home, that I'm alive, that I'm not getting shot at tonight.

After a while, I got on the radio myself.

"You know, we're sitting here tonight bitching about being on the side of a hill for hours, and meanwhile I have friends in Iraq who are worrying about getting shot at and making it to the next camp alive," I said. "Ya'll ought to have another look at that snow. It's a wonderful sight."

That shut 'em up for a while, but only for a while. Pretty soon they were replying to me, asking me questions, thanking me for going to Iraq to help the troops, expressing their support for our soldiers, and pretty much telling me that I was right—that all things considered, being stuck on a highway in the United States of America was not the worst thing in the world.

Of course, I knew that already.

I started a new Yahoo group in December for civilian contractors like myself who were back in the States and having a hard time adjusting. I found that drivers needed a place to share their thoughts and complaints, because unlike the troops, we didn't get any professional help at home for combat-related stress. Civilian counselors aren't trained to handle this and we did not have access to military counselors.

We had only each other. Our families couldn't understand. Nobody really understood. I constantly felt out of place and alone. Meanwhile, the press and other Americans seemed to regard us all as money-hungry mercenaries. They just didn't get it.

In my first post to the group, I explained who I was, and why I wanted to reach out to other people like me. I wrote that many people I knew had a hard time talking to noncontractors about our work in Iraq. "They give you funny looks and always assume that the only reason that you went was for the money," I wrote. Yes, the money was nice, I wrote, but I love my country and my family had always supported the military. And I added what I told Kenny months and months ago, when I was getting ready to go to Iraq. "I am going because one day someone will be doing this for you," I told him then. "So, today, I'm doing this for someone else's son or daughter."

That's how I felt then, and that was how I felt in December 2004, as Kenny was getting ready to leave for

Iraq himself. And I knew that the promise I made to my son would continue to be hard to keep. As much as I loved trucking, it no longer held the excitement it once had for me.

It got to the point that I stopped telling most people I met on the road about being in Iraq. That wasn't easy to do, but I had to do it. But in mid-December, I pulled into a truck stop in Little Rock, Arkansas, and got into a conversation with another driver while I was browsing in a chrome shop. I mentioned to him that I hadn't been in such a place in over a year. He asked why, and I told him: "I've been in Iraq."

His eyes lit up. That was a good sign. I had seen the opposite reaction too many times. He asked me what I had done there, and I explained that I had been a civilian contractor and a convoy commander. With that, an older gentleman interrupted, came up to me, and stuck out his hand. "I just want to shake your hand," he said. "Thank you for what you did."

I explained that I wasn't a soldier, I was just a truck driver. "I heard that," he said. "And I still wanted to say thanks."

I just stood there, not knowing what to think or say. There was something about the look in his eye, and firmness of his handshake, that got to me. I felt so much better. I didn't go to Iraq to get thanks, but this one really meant something.

During that weekend I spent with Kenny at Fort Hood before he shipped out, I showed him and a friend of his, a corporal, some of the video I took during our trip to Fallujah. The footage included scenes from the lake adjacent to the camp, and it showed some of my guys and some of the troops fooling around, talking to the camera, and taking a rare dip in the water.

As we sat in my truck and watched the video, I noticed that Kenny's friend was very quiet. He left the truck with my son after the video, and then returned to speak with me. He told me that by sheer coincidence, he had served with one of the soldiers in my video. That soldier, the corporal said, had been killed in Fallujah four days ago.

I didn't remember the soldier's name. Perhaps I never knew it. But I remembered him vividly. I remembered so much from that day—the lake, the singing, the horsing around. It was one of the best days I spent in a camp, and the troops were terrific. They were everything you'd want in an American soldier: Brave, generous, and determined to get the job done.

This young solider wasn't the first person I had met,

CYNTHIA I. MORGAN

however briefly, who lost his life in Iraq. And I knew he wouldn't be the last, because I had met so many soldiers and contractors during my time there. It would be too much to expect that everybody else I met would come home in one piece.

Later that night I put together clips of the soldier and copied them onto two disks—one for Kenny's friend, and one for the family of the dead soldier. I wanted his family to see him having fun, and to see that there was some joy in his life while he was in Iraq. If he were my son, I'd want to know that.

I was in tears as I edited the clip. Whatever else I loved about my time in Iraq, this part of the job really sucked.

For the first time in many years, I had Christmas dinner at my Mamaw's house. That had been a tradition when I was much younger, but once children and grandchildren scattered, the tradition died away. She brought it back in 2004.

My two other boys were with me, but there was an empty place where Kenny would have sat. He was in Iraq.

In early January 2005, I was on the road in Utah, driving hundreds of miles on roads covered in snow and ice. Once again, the landscape looked wonderful to me. The United States looked wonderful to me, in ways I never appreciated before I went to Iraq.

I sent a post to my Yahoo group on January 7, admitting to my friends in cyberspace that I just couldn't come to terms with my old life, my old way of life.

I wrote:

> I really want to go back to Iraq. Driving here is boring to me now. Several of the guys have said that driving trucks in the States has not changed, I have. I am beginning to see that they are right. I didn't think I had changed that much while I was gone, but I guess I have. And driving across the country brings mixed emotions for me. In one way, I am happy to be back. I am happy that I survived my year in Iraq, to be able to have the privilege to drive across 800 miles of ice and snow-

CYNTHIA I. MORGAN

and attending meetings, I volunteered to go out on a mission right away, as in the following day. So I got on the road, and it felt like I had never left.

I ran into several friends on my first few missions, which gave me a chance to catch up on things. I also met some guys whose wives were part of my Yahoo group. It was terrific to put a face to names I recognized.

It poured in late April and early May. When the rain stopped, somebody turned on the heat—it was a hundred and ten degrees by mid-May. Worse, it wasn't desert dry. It was a humid hundred and ten degrees. Brutal. Now you know why I liked seeing all that snow in Utah!

At around this time, I was assigned a mission along the route where my driver was wounded and I had taken some shrapnel in that last ambush before I was fired. After eight months of reliving that attack, this mission was extremely important to me. I knew that if I couldn't handle the trip—the anxiety, the awful memories—I wouldn't be able to handle any other dangerous mission. Then I'd have to go home, or just drive around Kuwait. I had to make it through this mission.

I was pretty calm as we pulled out of Scania, bound for Anaconda via Baghdad. I knew myself well enough to know that I could contain my emotions when the pressure was on. Afterward was another story.

We made our way through Baghdad at the beginning of rush hour. Yes, despite what you might read or hear about Iraq, life often looks pretty normal there. Most everybody just wants to get on with their lives. They go to work, do their jobs, and go home in rush-hour traffic.

Getting slowed down in traffic wasn't bad, considering that there were no bombs, no bullets, no rocket-propelled grenades, no mortars. Somebody threw some rocks at us by Taji, but that was no big deal.

I saw the overpass where I had seen that flash of light, where somebody had fired a bullet that hit Robert. It was quiet now.

I got through the overpass, through the area where I had to ram cars to get my guys through.

We got to Anaconda without a problem. While I was in the yard, struggling with some equipment, I heard a man's voice yelling, "Cindy!" I had heard that voice before, many times, but I couldn't place it at first. I turned around and saw somebody in a truck, half hanging out the passenger-side window. He was yelling and waving at me.

It was Roy!

The truck he was in came to an abrupt stop, and Roy

dove out and ran toward me with his arms wide open and a big smile on his face. He picked me up, twirled me around, and gave me the biggest hug I had had in a long time.

The last time I saw Roy, he was being taken away on a stretcher toward a chopper. We had talked a couple of times while I was in the States, but this was the first time I had seen him since he took a bullet in the leg. After we laughed and talked a bit, he rolled up his pants and showed me his scar: an entrance wound on one side of his knee, and an exit wound on the other. They were nasty scars, but in a way they were beautiful, too. They were beautiful because if Roy could show them off, it meant that Roy was alive and well.

"I'm glad you're back," Roy said. "This is where you belong."

His saying that told me that Roy believed I had done right by him when he was shot. Others had told me that, but hearing Roy's approval, well, that's what mattered most. After doubting myself, I was now at peace about that night when Roy was shot.

Weeks went by and I still hadn't seen Kenny. He was at BIAP, and the Iraqi Express—our nickname for the flatbed missions I was assigned to—wasn't running there. We were driving only between Kuwait and Anaconda or TQ/Ridgeway, the two major transportation hubs. If I was going to get a chance to see Kenny, I'd have to get on another assignment. That came at the end of May, when I got a chance to fill in for a driver who hauled heavy equipment. The heavy equipment trnasporters, or HETs as we called them, made the run to BIAP. It was dangerous work, and harder work, and dirtier work, but I didn't mind.

In mid-June, I got the mission I was hoping for—a drive to BIAP. And none too soon. Kenny was due to fly to Kuwait in a day or two.

On the night we were scheduled to push out, a dust storm blew in and we had to stay behind the wire. We were going to leave the following day, but not before I exchanged a few IMs with Kenny. We set up a time and place to meet later that day.

Then, nothing. The camp was locked down, so we were stuck behind the wire. And Kenny was back at BIAP, expecting to see me come rolling in.

By now, everybody from the other drivers to our escorts knew that Kenny was a soldier, based at BIAP. They also knew it had been six months since he'd left the States, and that I was dying to see him. They were all rooting for us to get moving so I could get there before

Kenny flew to Kuwait for his two-week leave. The escort unit's sergeant was a big help. When I saw him come back from a meeting during the lockdown and noticed that he didn't come straight to my truck, I had a bad feeling. I figured if the sergeant had good news, he'd have come right to me.

I was hanging out with some other guys who knew how anxious I was. They pushed me to go see the sergeant and find out what was going on. As I approached him, he hung his head and shook it. It took all I had not to break down and cry on the spot. We were still on lockdown. The only good news was that if the lockdown was lifted during the night we'd get rolling right away.

I was going to miss Kenny. I could feel it. I had come all this way just to miss my son by a few hours.

I told my guys we weren't rolling, and then I went to my truck so I could cry without anybody seeing me. I said a little prayer that we'd somehow get out on the road soon.

Not long afterward, I heard the sergeant's voice on the radio, telling all of us that we'd be rolling soon and that we had to get to our pre-mission briefing. He rolled up next to me, stopped, and smiled—the biggest smile I ever saw on any soldier in Iraq. I asked him if he had something to do with us getting out so quickly. He gave me a hug.

After the briefing, I was raring to go—and everybody

noticed. One soldier took a look at me and said, "Do you have a hot date or something?"

"I do," I said. "With my son."

Kenny and I had arranged to meet at a certain place, and at a certain time. If I wasn't there, he'd come back in a few hours. But with our delay getting out of camp, the timetable got screwed up. When we pulled into BIAP, the guys I drove with said they'd take care of my trailer, so I was free to hurry over to where I thought we said we'd meet, but it was the wrong place. When I finally found the right place, Kenny was nowhere to be seen.

It was well after midnight, and I had no idea where my son was. I ran into a few soldiers on patrol and we got to talking. I mentioned my son's name. "Specialist Elliott is one of my guys," a sergeant said. "Let me go get him."

I stayed put with a couple of my guys while the sergeant went to retrieve Kenny. We made small talk until the sergeant's voice came over the radio.

"What state is the subject from," the sergeant asked. I told him.

They had the wrong Specialist Elliott.

The sergeant could tell I was just about heartbroken. I told him what little information I had about where Kenny's quarters were. He said he'd try to track him down. Long minutes went by until we heard the sergeant on the radio again. They found him, and this time, it was the right Specialist Elliott.

I was walking toward my bobtail when I saw a Humvee approaching in the darkness. I knew Kenny would be in there, and he was. He stepped out and gave me a beautiful hug. God, he looked so good! Then he stepped back and said, "Well, we're even now, Mom. I've been shot at, too."

We spent hours talking, Kenny and I. I couldn't remember the last time we had spent this much time together, just the two of us, and the stars in the sky.

Later on, I got to meet the guys in Kenny's platoon, and he got a chance to meet the crew I was running with—including the sergeant who made our meeting happen.

Kenny brought me to one of his buddies. "I want you to meet my mom," he said.

His buddy's jaw dropped. He looked at me, and at Kenny, in complete disbelief. "We *are* in Iraq, right," he said. It was hysterical.

Eventually, I had to get back to the convoy, and Kenny had his own work to do. We gave each other another big hug. Neither of us knew if our paths would cross again anytime soon.

At that moment, I wasn't a truck driver in Iraq. I was the proud mom of an American soldier.

Kenny and I stayed in touch electronically through the summer of 2005. We IM'd each other early one morning in mid-August as Kenny was getting ready to go out on an extended patrol. Of course I was worried, but I tried to put it out of my mind.

That afternoon, as I was pulling into the yard after a local mission, my cell phone rang.

"Is this Ms. Morgan?" a voice asked. The voice did not sound familiar, which was odd and suddenly very scary.

"Yes, it is."

"I was told to call you because nobody else will," the unfamiliar voice said. "Your son has been hurt."

Oh my God.

"How bad? Where is he? Is it life-threatening?" I fumbled for questions.

"It's not life-threatening," the voice said. "He is not being sent to Germany." Seriously wounded soldiers were sent to Army facilities in Germany. That was good news.

"Okay," I said, letting out a sigh of relief. "Then how bad is it?"

"Ma'am, I can't tell you more than that. I am not supposed to be making this call and could get in trouble for it."

"Okay," I said. "Tell me what you can. How do I find out more?" I was desperate for more information, although at least I believed that Kenny's life was not in danger. Still, lots of wounds are not life-threatening, but certainly are life-altering.

"Ma'am, that is all I can tell you," the voice said again. "You will get a call in a few days." The voice hung up.

I knew there was no point trying to reach Kenny directly since even if he was okay, he was out of touch on patrol.

I called some friends and contacts in the military and they promised to find out what they could, if they could. But they also warned me that the call I had received was unofficial—it could be a hoax, they said. A hoax? Who would do such a thing? I couldn't imagine that.

I didn't tell anybody at home a thing about this, because I didn't want them to be worried. I talked to the Red Cross—the computers were down, so the people there couldn't check to see if Kenny was receiving treatment. I talked with a chaplain, who said he would try to get more information, but that it would take a couple of days.

I had a lieutenant I knew check the casualty lists. I asked every military person I knew to please find out what was going on. And I cried, and I screamed, and I went out of my mind.

The longest few days I spent in Iraq dragged on, until one afternoon I returned from a short local mission, signed on to my computer, and noticed that Kenny was signed on in Yahoo messenger. I nearly fell out of my chair. I sent him a message telling him what I had heard. He replied in an instant: He was fine.

It was a hoax, after all.

Kenny was furious and said he would inform his commanding officer about the call. I spent an hour calling people to tell them that Kenny was okay. All the while, and even now, I found it hard to believe that somebody could be so cruel, so hateful.

I later learned that I was not the first victim of such a hoax—families of soldiers and contractors alike have been subjected to this sort of torture.

I kept it together for as long as I could, and then I had a good long cry.

My contract with IAP expired in late August 2005. It was time for me to leave again, along with many of my friends whose contracts had also expired. I packed my stuff into footlockers to be shipped home. In my flat, four stark white walls stared back at me, walls that used to be decorated with tapestries, pictures, and a couple of hand-painted wall fans. A mirror lay in the foyer, wrapped in a blanket.

I stood at a window overlooking the Persian Gulf, and remembered the mornings I had spent watching the sun rise over that shimmering body of water.

In the preceding days, I had exchanged telephone numbers and email addresses with new friends, all of us promising to stay in touch, some of us actually believing that we would. My colleagues at IAP were from many nations—England, Australia, Wales, New Zealand, and South Africa, among others. Some were staying on in hopes of finding work with another company. Me? I was taking the vacation to Malaysia I had planned to take with Ed before I was fired by KBR, before Ed disappeared from my life.

After returning to the States from my trip to Malaysia, I flew back to Kuwait in late 2005. I've been working in Kuwait and Iraq ever since.

I am no longer the person I was when I arrived in Kuwait the first time, but then again, that was the plan. Of course I've changed. How could I not have? Just a couple of years ago, I was trapped in an abusive marriage, a prisoner of my insecurities—I was an emotional wreck.

Since I left behind my old life and started a new one, I've been tested in ways I couldn't have imagined when I walked out of that hotel room in Utah and watched the police take away my husband. I believe I have passed those tests.

I've undergone personal trauma: I've been shot, shot at, and sexually assaulted. I've been scared. I've been heartbroken. I've learned to become very cautious, almost paranoid, about men who try to get to know me. Are they destined to break my heart, again? I've yet to figure that one out. But I have not surrendered to despair and hopelessness, as I might have years ago, before I decided to live my life and not merely survive it.

I am not as naive as I used to be about the world we live in. Like many Americans, I used to believe that events overseas didn't affect me, and so there was no reason to pay attention. We're so busy, after all, with our own lives and our own problems. I was wrong about that. And anybody who still thinks that we can sit back and ignore the rest of the world really doesn't get it.

On a personal level, I've learned about the power all of us have to affect the lives of others, even strangers. Several people have told me that they would not have gone to work in Kuwait and Iraq if they hadn't read my website or joined my discussion group. A woman told me that I inspired her to get out of an abusive marriage.

I learned, too, that little decisions can have profound

and unintended consequences. If I hadn't insisted on driving on the night of that last ambush, if I had been in the passenger's seat where KBR wanted the CC to be sitting, my driver would not have gotten shot. The bullet would have crashed into my leg, not his. How's that for guilt?

From my perspective, the United States is doing right by the people of Iraq. Our troops are not conquerors, but liberators, and I'm proud of the small part I'm playing in helping them. I won't deny that terrible things have taken place—I've seen what war does to the human body and the human spirit. But I believe, in the end, the Iraqi people will emerge from this trial better off than they were under Saddam.

Today, awful news travels faster than ever before, so the press instantly shows us pictures of the latest suicide bombing or attack, and Americans are horrified. But the violence is only one part of the story in Iraq—the only part most people hear about. Where are the reports about the schools under construction, the power plants and water-treatment plants we are helping to build?

Seeing this side of the war has made me even more of a patriot. Seeing the effects of Saddam's rule in Iraq reminds me—not that I needed a reminder—that we're lucky to live in a nation like ours, with freedoms we take for granted but others around the world can only dream about. We can speak out against the government without being thrown into prison. We don't live in a war zone. We have the right to be treated equally before the law. And if we're down on our luck, as I know firsthand, we have government programs to help us get back on our feet.

I get annoyed when I hear parents of our soldiers saying that their children joined the military not to fight, but to get money for college. Excuse me? My son Kenny wanted to be a soldier since he was old enough to walk and talk—not just because of the perks, but because he considered the military an honorable way to serve his country. The military is not about just getting money for college. It's not a free ride to a better life. It is an institution that defends our freedom, pure and simple. I'm proud of my son Kenny, an Army Cavalry Scout. I'm proud to be the sister of a former Navy submariner, the niece of a Vietnam vet, and the granddaughter and grand-niece of World War II vets. They joined the service not because they wanted a free education, but because they believe in our country and our way of life.

When my son told me he was signing up for the Army, I told him he'd better understand what he was getting into. I told him he could be sent to a war, and he might not come back. He said he understood that, and that he wanted to join anyway. Yes, I'm scared for him. And yes, I support him a hundred percent.

We live in a dangerous world. I'm not sure if I understood that before, but I do now. I know something about cruelty and evil—but I refused to give in to the belief that somehow most people are bad. To believe that is to give up all hope of making the world, or our small part of it, better. I still have that hope.

I used to think, as I saw the world's miseries played out on television, that there is very little one person can do about the world's injustices. I don't believe that anymore. No, I can't change the world by myself, but I can make a difference in a few lives, and maybe they'll make a difference in the lives of people I'll never meet. And that's how you change the world.

In the end, I believe love will triumph over hate. And we are on the right side.

ACKNOWLEDGMENTS

TO MY FAMILY FOR GIVING ME
their love and support in spite of their
fear for my safety..

In life, many people will cross our paths. Many will go
unnoticed, and many others will walk along with us for a

while. I wish to say thank you to these folks for walking the path with me.

Jack Griffie, Richard Borma, Ed Burleson, and Earl Shank for being the best friends a girl could have for so many years and for sticking with me through it all, good and bad.

Steven Antill, Mike Kelly, Kevin Toomey, "Tiger Six," and Jana Crowder, for being my sounding board when things got crazy and confusing.

Mickey "Hollywood" Holloway, for giving me your trust and for showing me that not all men are pigs.

Roy Hawkins, for showing me what true courage is.

Robert Rowe, wherever you are, I hope that your leg has healed well.

Keith Nash, for telling me about the jobs in Iraq supporting our troops. This has changed my life.

"Ed," no matter the outcome, you were there when I really needed a friend.

The guys that ran in my convoys—no CC could have asked for a better crew or friends. Thanks for your support and for trusting me.

All the military units that ran escort for me and my guys, thank you so much for covering our tails.

The unnamed soldier from the 1/86th FA, you are and always will be my hero. Thank you for "just doing your job." I am glad you made it home safely.

Terry Golway, thank you for taking my thoughts, feelings, and words and helping me smooth them all out into something I can be proud of.

Margaret Riley, Eva Gardos, and Jason Blum, thank you for talking me into writing this book and being such great support. This would never have happened if not for ya'll.

Liz Stein, for your wonderful editing skills and for listening to my ramblings. You have taught me a lot.

Maris Kreizman, for all the behind the scenes work. I know I tried your patience at times.

To all the staff of the publicity department at Free Press, for the hard work put in and for pushing this out ahead of time.

Members of "American Contractors in Iraq" and other Yahoo support groups, I have never seen many of your faces, but you have been some of the greatest support and encouragement I have gotten through it all. Thank you!

To all civilian contractors, keep up the good work in supporting our guys and gals in the military, and our country; it is a thankless job and you do it well.

To our military personnel and their families, thank you for your sacrifice. You serve our great country with honor.

To Darren Eccleston, Joel Ferro, Tillman "Lee" Nelson, Andy Smith, Ken Blalock, Greg Martin, Robert Easley, Chris Roberts, Chris Larson, Larry Cox, John

Peay, Tracy Mason, Tim, Willain "Woody" Woodward, Sean Laevenz, Ben Davis, Charles Wilkinson, Dennis Hamilton, Raymond Lehr, David Mongeau, George Prescott, Jerry Hill, John "Roster" Faulkner, Ted Watcher, Mike Collier, Joe Swanson, Nathan Frame, Billy More, Ray Wilding, Vern Fulkerson, Ben Gay, Dave "Taz" Ford, Richard Daviss, JJ Erasmus, Ken O'Donoghue, Darren Camburn, Mike Engelbrech, Shawn Carter, Emmett McCall, Shad Perry, Troy Mills, Bill Baker, and all the others . . . I thank you. Ya'll know when and what for and for making my time in Iraq what it was, good and bad. . . . A wonderful experience that I will never forget!

ABOUT THE AUTHOR

CYNTHIA MORGAN drove a big rig across the United States for twelve years before venturing into the war zone of Iraq in 2003, where she was a civilian convoy commander in charge of up to thirty trucks delivering supplies to American bases throughout the war-torn country. After six months back in the United States, she returned to Iraq in 2005. She lives, usually, in Tennessee.